James Sprunt

Tales and traditions of the lower Cape Fear

1661-1896

James Sprunt

Tales and traditions of the lower Cape Fear
1661-1896

ISBN/EAN: 9783337074494

Printed in Europe, USA, Canada, Australia, Japan

Cover: Foto ©ninafisch / pixelio.de

More available books at **www.hansebooks.com**

AND

TRADITIONS

OF THE

LOWER CAPE FEAR,

1661-1896.

By JAMES SPRUNT

Entered according to Act of Congress in the year of 1896, by JAMES SPRUNT, in the office of the Librarian of Congress at Washington.

WILMINGTON, N. C.
LeGwin Brothers, Printers.

1896.

TO THE MEMORY

OF

GEORGE DAVIS,

WHO, EVER UPHOLDING THE HONOR OF HIS NATIVE LAND,

MODESTLY EXEMPLIFIED IN HIS LONG, EVENTFUL LIFE

AND

STAINLESS REPUTATION,

THE IDEAL PATRIOT, JURIST, STATESMAN ;

AND ABOVE ALL,

THE NOBLE CHRISTIAN GENTLEMAN,

THIS HUMBLE RECORD

OF HIS BELOVED CAPE FEAR

IS AFFECTIONATELY AND REVERENTLY INSCRIBED.

PREFACE.

THIS little guide book, prepared perhaps too hastily, was undertaken six weeks ago as a compliment to Captain John W. Harper, of the Steamer "Wilmington," by one who treasures the memories of the Lower Cape Fear, and who has tried to catch the vanishing lines of its history and traditions for the benefit of those who may not be unmindful of the annals of a brave and generous people.

WILMINGTON, N. C., 1ST MAY, 1896.

TABLE OF CONTENTS.

	PAGE
The Southport Steamer	9
The First Steamboat on Cape Fear River	12
Settlement of Wilmington	15
Sanitary	16
Cape Fear Steamboats	18
Negro Head Point	20
Hilton Park	23
Market Dock and Ferry	24
Colonial Governor's Residence	28
Confederate States Cotton Press	30
Historic Mansion	31
United States Monitor Nantucket	32
Old Ship Yard	33
The Dram Tree	35
Hospital Point	36
Brunswick River, Mallory Creek and Clarendon Plantation	38
Old Town Settlement	38
Big Island	39
Rice Birds	39
First Navigators of the Cape Fear—King Watcoosa and his Daughters	40
Cushing's Exploits	43
Cushing's Daring Visit to Fort Anderson	46
Carolina Beach	48
Gander Hall	49
Sedgeley Abbey	50
First White Settlement	52

TABLE OF CONTENTS—CONTINUED.

PAGE.

Cape Fear Indians	54
Lilliput	55
Kendal	58
Orton	61
Colonial Governor Tryon's Palace—Scene of the First Outbreak of the Revolutionary War	67
Ruins of Brunswick	72
Ruins of St. Philip's Church	73
Colonial Ferry and Inn	75
Confederate Fortifications	77
Fort Anderson	78
A Colonial Fort	80
Fort Fisher	83
Description of Situation	83
Land Face of Fort Fisher	86
Sea Face of Fort Fisher	88
The Fort Fisher Fight	90
Craig's Landing	97
The Heroine of Confederate Point	98
Butler's Powder Ship	107
The Rocks—Closure of the Inlet	109
Battery Lamb—Confederate Salt Works	111
Snow Marsh—Dredging Steamer "Cape Fear"	112
Price's Creek Lighthouse Confederate States Signal Station	114
Wilmington and Charleston Mail Boats	117
Cape Fear Quarantine Station	119
Southport—Governor Smith—Cape Fear Pilots	122
Bald Head Pirates	125
Fort Caswell	128
Evacuation and Explosion of Fort Caswell	131
War Department Records—Forts Johnston and Caswell	134
Fort Johnston, North Carolina	135

TABLE OF CONTENTS—CONCLUDED.

PAGE.

Wild Pigeons—Wreck of Spanish Ship—Probable Murder—Treasure Trove 140
Life Savers 143
A Run to Sea 144
Captain Fry and the Cuban War 145
Cape Fear Privateers in the War of 1812 and 1861 154
Blockade Runners 162
Maffitt's Experience 166
Blockade Runner "Don" 184
Pilots in a Storm 205
Homeward Bound 213

Advertisements .... I to LXII

The Southport Steamer.

THE steamer "Wilmington" is a model of marine architecture, combining spacious and comfortable passenger accommodations with the greatest speed attained by steam craft on the Cape Fear river. Her clean decks and tidy saloons afford the bracing outside air, or the restful seclusion which invites repose. The daily run to and from Southport is made in two hours, including all river landings; and the object of this little book is to interest and amuse the traveller by a concise description of Wilmington business enterprise and local scenery, contrasting the record of the present busy age with the history and traditions of long ago.

As we approach the gangway of this stately steamer, we are impressed with the quiet of the scene. We miss, most gratefully, the noisy roar of escaping steam, the confusing shouts, the imprecations and jostlings of the professional baggage-smasher, and all the other distasteful and offensive features of former days. We are promptly met by the Commander and owner, a dignified, stalwart specimen of the American sailor and gentleman, who receives us courteously, and who welcomes us with unmistakable cordiality. His name is John W. Harper, and he is said to be the favorite skipper of North Carolina. When you have made the round trip in his charge you will not doubt his title to that honorable distinction. A successful steamboat captain should be competent, cool, cautious, patient, polite and amiable to the last degree; with an infinite reserve stock of never failing good humor. These attributes are possessed by Captain Harper, to an unusual extent, which combined with a large experience, inspire confidence and insure safety. He has been running boats up and down the river for twenty-two years, and he has made, during that time, more than thirteen thousand trips between Wilmington and Southport—equal to fifteen trips around the world. He was the pioneer of the regular summer excursions to the Cape Fear seacoast, by which thousands of weary people and sick babies from the up country and the city, oppressed with mid-summer heat, have been refreshed and strengthened by ocean breezes and salt water at a nominal expense. It is a matter of fact that salt sea air will often do more good to a sick, puny child than any of the medical remedies in the pharmacopœia. Many anxious, worn-out mothers, have had reason to bless Captain Harper as the means under Providence of restoring to health their sick or feeble little ones. A beloved physician has often said that daily trips from Wilmington to Southport are even more beneficial to sick children than a residence on the seashore. The gliding motion of the boat soothes them, the clear, fresh air of the river invigorates and strengthens them, and the entire freedom from dust and grime which is so disagreeable and hurtful on railroad journeys brings grateful sensations of cleanliness and comfort to young and old alike.

"How happy they
 Who from the toil and tumult of their lives
 Steal to look down where naught but ocean strives."

The First Steamboat on the Cape Fear River.

Let us contrast the swift steamer Wilmington with the ridiculous example of former days—let us turn back for three-quarters of a century, when the town of Wilmington contained only a tenth of its present population, and recall an incident, related to the writer by our venerable townsman, Col. J. G. Burr, which created the greatest excitement at the time, and which was the occasion of the wildest exuberance of feeling among the usually staid inhabitants of the town—the arrival of the first steamboat in the Cape Fear River. A joint stock company had been formed for the purpose of having one built to ply between Wilmington and Smithville or Wilmington and Fayetteville. Captain Otway Burns, of Privateer "Snap Dragon" fame, during the war of 1812, was the contractor. The boat was built at Beaufort, where he resided. When the company was informed that the steamer was finished and ready for delivery, they despatched Captain Thomas N. Gautier, an old sea captain, and a worthy citizen of the town, to take command and bring her to her destined port. Expectations were on tiptoe after the departure of the Captain; a feverish excitement existed in the community, which daily increased, as nothing was heard from him for a time, owing to the irregularity of the mails; but early one morning this anxiety broke into the wildest enthusiasm when it was announced that the "Prometheus" was in the river and had turned the Dram Tree. Bells were rung, cannon fired, and the entire population, without regard to age, sex or color, thronged the wharves to welcome her arrival. The tide was at the ebb, and the struggle between the advancing steamer and the fierce current was a desperate one; for she panted fearfully, as though wind-blown and exhausted; she could be seen in the distance, enveloped in smoke, and the scream of her high pressure engine reverberated through the woods, while she slowly but surely crept along. As she neared Market Dock, where the steamer Wilmington is at present moored, the old Captain, gorgeously arrayed in brilliant uniform, with cocked hat and epaulettes, made his appearance near the engine room, in full view of the excited crowd, and applying his speaking-trumpet, his symbol of authority, to his lips, bellowed to the engineer below, in a voice that sounded like the roar of some hoarse monster of the deep: "Give it to her, Snyder"; and while Snyder gave her all the steam she could bear, the laboring "Prometheus" snorted by amid the cheers of the excited multitude. In those days the river traffic was sustained by sailing sloops and small schooners, with limited passenger accommodations and less comfort. The schedule time to Smithville (now called Southport), was four hours, wind and weather permitting, and the fare was one dollar each way.

Settlement of Wilmington.

About the year 1730, some five years after the town of Brunswick was established fourteen miles lower down the river, a few settlers built their humble habitations on a bluff in the midst of the primeval forest now known as Dickinson Hill, nearly opposite the junction of the Northeast and Northwest branches of the Cape Fear river, which was then known as the Clarendon river. Their purpose was to find a safer harbor than the exposed roadstead of Brunswick, and to secure a larger share of the river traffic from the up country, which was then very profitable.

In a few months this hamlet increased to the proportion of a small village, without order or regularity, which was named New Liverpool.

In 1733 it was surveyed into town lots, although the inhabitants had no legal right to the land.

In the same year John Watson obtained a Royal grant of 640 acres of land on the East side of the Northeast branch of the river called the Cape Fear, in which was included the site of the village or town called New Liverpool, but latterly known as Newton.

In 1739, through the influence of the Colonial Governor, Gabriel Johnston, the name was again changed to

Wilmington, in honor of Spencer Compton, Baron Wilmington, an influential English friend of the Governor. In 1760 King George II. made the town a borough, with the right of sending a member to the Assembly.

Arthur Dobbs was then the Royal Governor, and he lived at Russelboro, which is now a part of Orton plantation.

In 1763, George III. being King, additional rights were granted by the Crown, the corporate title being made "The Mayor, Recorder and Aldermen of the Borough of Wilmington."

In 1776 the corporate name was changed to that of "The Commissioners of the Town of Wilmington"; and this name was continued for one hundred years. The present corporate name, "The City of Wilmington," was acquired in the year 1866.

Sanitary.

ARTIFICIAL drainage has in recent years carried the storm water from the city into the tributary streams of the Cape Fear, and if maintained in proper condition, is well designed to effectually drain a large area which was formerly the most unhealthy quarter of the settlement. As a result malarial fever has greatly decreased in the last twenty years, and it may be truly said, although stigmatized forty years ago as the sailor's grave, and shunned by the people of the up country as an unsafe place in which to tarry all night during the summer and autumn, it has become exceptionally healthy. As an evidence of this, the death-rate for several years past has been much smaller than in the surrounding country; and compares favorably with the most favored towns of its size on the Atlantic coast—the annual death-rate being about seventeen to the thousand.

Drainage has not, and cannot, it is true, alter the malarial influence upon crews of vessels sleeping on the river in the months of July, August, September and October. This standing menace to the prosperity of our shipping, as evidenced by the scarcity of tonnage during these months, has been seriously considered for many years, and a remedy actually devised. The difficulty has been to impress the lesson of prevention, learned at such a cost, upon the interested parties. The State Board of Health has done much towards inculcating important advice upon the subject. For many years it has been known, as well by the people as by the doctors, that the fevers occurring among the vessels in our tide-water streams were preventable in a marked degree.

Observations extending over a space of time marked by four or five generations demonstrated that the cause of sickness among sailors was due very largely to sleeping on board of vessels in the Cape Fear river particularly. This fact was so firmly established in the opinion of merchants in Wilmington, that $20,000 was subscribed to build a home for seamen, in which they might find a safe retreat from the effluvia of the river, and what is not exactly pertinent to the present subject, to escape also the abominable effluvia of low sailor lodgings. In this building ample provision was made for more sailors than ever visit the port of Wilmington at one time, and by the Christian benevolence of Capt. Gilbert Potter, one of the oldest citizens of our city, who had himself been a sea-captain, a house of worship, supplied by the yearly ministrations of a preacher, was provided, to throw around these "toilers of the sea" a beneficent influence.

Cape Fear Steamboats.

BEFORE railroads were so numerous and the means of transportation limited, the Cape Fear River Steamboat Company enjoyed a large share of public patronage. The merchandise for the merchants of Western North Carolina, East Tennessee and portions of South Carolina,

Georgia and Virginia was brought to this port by vessels, transferred to the river boats to Fayetteville, and then forwarded to destination by the slow, tedious and expensive means of transportation by wagons. Fayetteville in those days was a place of as much business and importance in a commercial point of view as any inland town in the country, and every citizen in the place took pride in seeing the place flourish and prosper. The merchants built steamboats and plank-roads, and in this way fostered the trade which from the position at the head of navigation was a natural outlet. But as soon as the railroad became the grand artery to receive and disperse everything as public and private interest directed, the river traffic decreased, and with its decline the plank-roads ceased to be profitable, and there was almost a total disappearance of the white-covered caravans that plied between the mountains and the Cape Fear country.

The Worths, Lutterlohs, Orrells and others had regular fleets on the Cape Fear. We now recall the steamers Rowan, Henrietta, Chatham, Gov. Graham, Flora McDonald, A. P. Hurt and Gov. Worth, commanded by captains Roderick McRae, A. P. Hurt, Sam Skinner, A. H. Worth; the steamers Brothers, James R. Grist, Douglass, J. T. Petteway and Scottish Chief, all of which boats were at times under the command of that whole-souled, jovial Scotchman, "Uncle Johnnie Banks"; the steamer Sun, Captain Rush; the steamer Enterprise, Captain Datus Jones; the Fannie Lutterloh, Captain Stedman; the Kate McLaurin, Captain Daily; the Black River, Captain Jesse Dicksey; the John Dawson, Captain Lawton; the Hattie Hart, Captain Peck; and other steamers and captains we cannot now recall. In these later days there has been employed in the river trade the steamers Murchison, the North State, the Cumberland, the Juniper, the Cape Fear, the Wave, the J. C. Stewart, the Frank Sessoms, commanded by captains Garrason, Smith, Green, Worth, McLauchlin and the Robesons.

Negro Head Point.

As the "Wilmington" lies at her wharf, near Market Dock, we see from her spacious upper deck Negro Head Point, which divides the waters of the Cape Fear into Northwest and Northeast branches. It is the Northern limit of the jurisdiction of the Board of Commissioners of Navigation and Pilotage, and its name is derived from a melancholy incident in the time of slavery.

In the latter part of the year 1831, through the influence of Northern emissaries, an insurrection of Negro slaves occurred in Southampton, Virginia, which spread rapidly into this State, creating great and general excitement.

A number of helpless white women and children fell victims to the madness of the blacks, which so infuriated the whites that a race war seemed inevitable. All the approaches to the town of Wilmington were heavily guarded by the militia, and two companies of United States troops, numbering 170 men, from Fortress Monroe, remained on duty here for several months. The uprising was overcome and the leaders suffered death. Four were hanged near Giblem Lodge, on Princess street; several others were shot, and, according to the barbarous custom of those days, their heads, after decapitation, were placed on poles in conspicuous places as a warning to others like minded.

At the intersection of Market and Front streets, a few rods from the steamer's dock, stood the town market house, where the slave-trade was constantly carried on until 1863.

We draw a veil over the sad scenes enacted there, but we recall the fact that it was not until after the slave-traders of the North had received full value of their human merchandise from their Southern brethren that our neighbors began to realize the enormity of the institution.

And yet our people who were impoverished by its downfall would not, if they could, deprive the negro of his freedom.

With reference to the introduction of slavery into Carolina by the Colonial Governor, Yeamans, from Barbadoes, in 1671, the late lamented George Davis said:

"This seems to be a simple announcement of a very commonplace fact; but it was the little cloud no bigger than a man's hand. It was the most portentous event of all our early history. For he carried with him from Barbadoes his negro slaves; and that was the first introduction of African slavery into Carolina.—(Bancroft, 2,170; Rivers, 169.)

"If, as he sat by the camp-fire in that lonely Southern wilderness, he could have gazed with prophetic vision down the vista of two hundred years, and seen the stormy and tragic end of that of which he was then so quietly inaugurating the beginning, must he not have exclaimed with Ophelia, as she beheld the wreck of her heart's young love:

"'O, woe is me! To have seen what I have seen, see what I see'"!

Hilton Park.

Just beyond Negro Head Point, on the Northeast branch, a beautiful wooded bluff may be seen. It is Hilton, named in honor of one of the three first explorers from Barbadoes who visited the Cape Fear in the year 1663, which became famous in Revolutionary history as the home of Cornelius Harnett, a prominent patriot of this section and a conspicuous, noted personage of his day. Until a few years ago his house, a neat Colonial structure, embowered by noble oaks, and subsequently owned by the Hill family, was our most interesting relic of Revolutionary times; but the estate passed into other hands, and this picturesque, historic home was demolished, to the shame of our people, who were offered the building, as a public gift, for the cost of its removal and preservation.

"A perfect woman, nobly planned," whose skill and virtues are of national reputation, and whose ancestors were always leaders on the Cape Fear, has happily devised, as President of the Society of Colonial Dames, the means of placing a public monument over the grave of this sturdy patriot whose dust long since mingled with its mother earth in old St. James' churchyard, ere his noble sacrifice of life to liberty was appropriately recognized.

Market Dock and Ferry.

The old Market Dock, at which the "Wilmington" is moored, is worthy of passing notice. During the Revolutionary war, while the town of Wilmington was in possession of the British troops under Major Craig, an American soldier in ambush on Point Petre or Negro Head shot with a long-range rifle a number of British troopers standing at Market Dock.

Also, more than a hundred years afterwards, when the Federal troops under Schofield and Terry reached the

Brunswick side of Market Dock ferry on their way to Wilmington, the last stand of the Confederate troops was made near Market Dock; a detachment of light artillery having fired from this point upon the advancing Federals on the west side of the river and checked their progress. The Federals were in overwhelming numbers, however, and the artillerists soon followed Bragg's retreating forces before the invaders reached the town.

The Confederates had carefully removed from the west shore all boats and other means of transportation to the Wilmington side in order to retard the Federal advance. Consequently there was considerable delay in crossing the river, which was at last overcome by a demented Wilmington woman, who secretly obtained a small boat and paddled it across to the Federals, by means of which other craft was soon floated, and the town for a second time invested by a hostile army.

In the early morning of the 22d February, 1865, a Confederate officer in command of the last battalion of infantry to leave Wilmington when evacuated by the Southern troops, was leading his men along Fourth street on his way to rejoin General Hoke, who had passed up to the North East River the night previous. Saddened and wofully depressed with the thought of leaving all his loved ones to the mercy of enemies, he called the next officer, and, giving him orders about the route to march, turned back from Boney Bridge to hurriedly bid adieu to all the dear ones. Passing down Red Cross to Front, hurried visits were made to several friends, but on reaching the intersection of Market and Front streets, the proximity of the enemy was apparent, for there were gathered the Mayor and Aldermen of the city—John Dawson, W. S. Anderson, P. W. Fanning and others of the citizens who had there met to turn over the keys of the city to the captors. Around on every side were seen the results of the cannon-firing of the day previous, the window-panes in every house were shattered and artillery debris lay scattered around. Immediate passing events urged a very prompt retreat, and the officer hurried to his father's house to say good-bye and to receive their loving blessings and wishes for safety. Hastening through this distressing scene, he began his journey to rejoin his command, accompanied as far as Boney Bridge by his sister. The streets of Pompeii or Herculaneum when buried beneath the lava of Vesuvius were no quieter than those of Wilmington. Not a soul was to be seen on the streets, not a window-blind but was closed. Apparently even the dogs were affected by the prevailing distress. The mournful walk was continued, and the officer, parting with his sister, continued his march with feelings easily to be imagined, and soon rejoined his command about five miles out. This lady subsequently said that this was the loneliest walk of her life-time. She met no one between Boney Bridge and her father's residence, South of Market street on Second street.

(Lord Cornwallis' Headquarters.)

Colonial Governor's Residence.

A FEW steps from the "Wilmington's" wharf is an unpretentious tobacconist's shop—a small brick building—which is said to have been the residence of the celebrated Colonial Governor, William Tryon, who was closely identified with the Cape Fear section of Revo-

(Confederate General's Headquarters.)

lutionary times, as will be seen further on. Higher up, on the corner of Third Street, may be seen the fine residence, which served as the headquarters of General Lord Cornwallis, commander of the British forces. It is now owned and occupied by Mrs. McRary. Immediately opposite stands an ancient residence of the DeRosset family, which was used throughout the civil war nearly a hundred years later as headquarters of the Confederate Generals commanding this district.

Confederate States Cotton Press.

As we leave the wharf, on our passage down the river, we see a conspicuous relic of an extraordinary era in the foreign trade of Wilmington. It is the leaning, but unbroken, brick chimney of the Confederate States Cotton Press established here in the year 1864. This press was the first in Wilmington, and had a capacity of 500 bales a day. The wharves and marsh adjoining to the warehouses were piled with enormous quantities of cotton bales belonging to the Confederate Government, and hither came all the swift blockade-runners for cargoes which were laden with great rapidity; work went on day and night, as many as twenty steamers loading together. The entire plant, together with several thousand bales of cotton was destroyed by fire by order of General Bragg upon his evacuation of this place on the evening of February 21st, 1865.

Historic Mansion.

ON the East bank at a considerable elevation above the river is an historic residence. It was built and occupied by the first Governor of North Carolina elected by the people, Edward B. Dudley, a statesman of liberal and patriotic views, of commanding presence and of most amiable manners. His name should ever be held in grateful remembrance by our people, for he was a leader in every public and private work for the benefit and prosperity of Wilmington, and contributed $25,000 towards the building of the Wilmington & Weldon Railroad, of which he was the first President. He was a man of generous impulses and stainless integrity, beloved and honored by rich and poor, and by white and black alike. He served as a member of the Twenty-first Congress, to which he was elected in the year 1829, but declined re-election, because he said Congress was not the place for an honest man.

In May, 1849, he entertained at this residence the distinguished Daniel Webster, who visited Wilmington as his guest. Mr. Webster was doubtless well cared for, as he wrote to a friend May 7th: "We are grandly lodged in the Governor's mansion."

In later years Cardinal Gibbons, with an Archbishop and twelve bishops were entertained here by Mr. Kerchner, who owned the place at that time.

The present owner and occupant has greatly enlarged and improved this property, at the foot of which may be seen the

United States Monitor Nantucket.

A battle-scarred survivor of the war between the States. This vessel took part in the bombardment of Fort Sumter and in other conflicts at sea. Her turret is indented by hostile shot and shell, and she is regarded as an interesting type of the old navy. The "Nantucket" is in charge of the Wilmington Division of North Carolina Naval Reserves, and is used as the school ship of this fine organization.

Old Ship-Yard.

THE first and only sailing ship built at Wilmington was launched June 5th, 1833, by Mr. John K. McIlhenny, and named after his two daughters, "Eliza and Susan." The work was done by Mr. Josh Toomer, the grandfather of the present generation of that name, under the direction of Mr. McIlhenny, at the saw mill of the latter upon the exact site of Kidder's mill. Mr. McIlhenny owned a rice mill and a saw mill, both of which were about the first erected at Wilmington.

The "Eliza and Susan" was a full-rig ship of 316 tons, built of the staunchest live oak, and of unusual strength. The oak came partly from Bald Head and partly from Lockwood's Folly. She was pine-planked and coppered. It is not certain what cargo she took out, but she came back loaded with salt. The commander was Captain Huntington, already in middle life at the time of the ship's first voyage. His son afterwards married Miss Brown of this place.

Long afterwards, while the "Eliza and Susan" was engaged in the whaling trade of the Pacific, Captain Thomas F. Peck, who had gone from Wilmington to the land of gold with the "forty-niners," saw the familiar Wilmington ship at anchor in San Francisco bay. He was subsequently invited on board and served with a glass of Cape Fear river water, then highly esteemed as pure and wholesome, which had been kept in one of the reserve tanks for more than twenty years.

At right angles with the river and parallel with Queen street Mr. McIlhenny cut a canal; at the head of this canal the ship was built. In launching her she stuck in the mud, and Colonel McIlhenny remembers as a boy seeing his father fume most vigorously about it. There were on the river about that time the "Enterprise," the "Spray," the "John Walker" and the "Henrietta." Mr. McIlhenny and Governor Dudley owned the "Enterprise," which was a very small boat, and was used by them for towing the rice flats from the different plantations. They lengthened her first ten or twelve feet, then afterwards gave her an additional length and ran her as a passenger boat from Wilmington to Smithville.

The "Spray" ran about 1853 or 1854, and was the fastest of them all. She was shaped something like a barrel, hooped up on the sides. She was the favorite steamboat plying between Wilmington and Smithville a few years before the war.

Mr. McIlhenny was awarded a contract by the Government to furnish timber for building the United States man-of-war "Pennsylvania." No large ships were built here subsequently. Mr. B. W. Beery built some schooners and pilot boats, and afterwards Mr. Cassidy established the ship-yard now conducted by Captain S. W. Skinner, the only ship-yard in Wilmington.

The Dram Tree.

Looking ahead to the farthest point in view, we distinguish an object, the passing of which was signalized in "ye olden time" by the popping of corks or by other demonstration of a convivial nature. It is an old cypress tree, moss-covered and battered by the storms of centuries. Like a grim sentinel, it stands to warn the out-going mariner that his voyage has begun.

and to welcome the in-coming storm-tossed sailor to
the quiet harbor beyond. Its name is significant. It
is called the Dram Tree, and it has borne this name for
more than a hundred years. For further particulars
see Captain Harper.

Hospital Point.

We now pass Hospital Point, whereon was placed a
pest house during the small-pox plague which followed
Sherman's army. Many thousands of negro refugees
fell victims to this dread disease. At low water may
be seen the charred remains of several Confederate
war vessels which composed Commodore Lynch's small
and crippled fleet, and which were burned by the Confederates when Wilmington was evacuated after the
fall of Fort Fisher.

This place is also known as Mount Tirzah, and it
is the property of the Seamen's Friend Society of
Wilmington. In 1835 the citizens of the town held a
meeting to establish the Wilmington Marine Hospital
for the benefit of sick seamen in this port for whom no
provision up to that time had been made. Subscriptions
were raised, a society formed, and the Mount Tirzah

property of 150 acres and several houses standing thereon purchased from Governor E. B. Dudley for one thousand dollars.

The principal building, a house of two stories, was converted into a hospital and managed by the Marine Hospital Society until April 24th, 1855, when this property and the other assets of the Society were transferred to the Seamen's Friend Society, which undertook to carry on the work in conjunction with its own benevolent enterprise in the port of Wilmington. Later on the United States Government established in the Southeastern part of the town a fine marine hospital, which provided greatly improved quarters and treatment for sick seamen, and which is now one of the most interesting features of the port of Wilmington.

The Mount Tirzah property is occasionally used by the City Government for the isolation and treatment of cases of infectious diseases.

Brunswick River—Mallory Creek— Clarendon Plantation.

ON the West side is the mouth of Brunswick River, still partly obstructed by Confederate torpedoes.

Mallory Creek is some distance lower down. Near it is "Clarendon," a fine rice plantation, originally owned by Marsden Campbell and afterwards the property of William Watters, Esq., a Cape Fear gentleman of the Old School, and a planter of large experience. It is now owned by Messrs. Fred Kidder and H. Walters.

Old Town Settlement.

PASSING Barnard's Creek on the East side, near which in the olden time were several valuable plantations, we come to Town Creek, where 800 colonists from Barbadoes, led by Sir John Yeamans, built a town in the year 1665 and called it Charlestown in honor of the reigning sovereign of England, King Charles II.

Sir John had been a loyal adherent of the deposed King, and was rewarded upon the Restoration with the order of Knighthood and a royal grant of lands in Carolina. He is said to have been the first British

Governor of Clarendon, which extended originally from Albemarle to St. Augustine, Florida. The settlement did not prosper. In a few years the colonists abandoned it and removed, some to Charleston, S. C., others to Albemarle, in the North. Not a white man remained, and the river land continued in possession of the Indians for many years after.

Big Island--Rice Birds.

About a mile below Old Town is Big Island, a tract of nearly 300 acres of rich alluvial soil, which the first voyagers to the Cape Fear in 1663 named Crane Island, and which is charted by the United States Coast Survey as Campbell's Island. It was formerly a light-house station, but the light was discontinued during the late war and a battery erected in its place. There is a fortune in this island waiting for some enterprising truck farmer, as the State Geologist says it contains some of the richest lands in the South, that will never need fertilizing. Millions of fat rice birds roost here at night after preying upon the milky rice of the neighboring plantations during the day. It is estimated that these toothsome little pests devour 25 per cent. of all the rice made on the Cape Fear. They appear every Fall together on the same day and depart during a single night when the rice gets too hard for them. The planters have never been able to protect their crops from the yearly ravages of these birds. Although a gang of boys and men are kept firing guns at them all day, a very small proportion of the immense droves is killed. For a dainty supper, a fat rice bird is perhaps the most delicious morsel that ever tickled the palate of an epicure.

First Navigators of the Cape Fear.
King Watcoosa and His Daughters.

The first reference made in history to Big Island is in the report of the Commissioners sent from Barbadoes in October, 1663, to explore the river Cape Fear.

After describing the voyage to the Cape, they say that the channel is on the East side by the Cape shore, and that it lies close aboard the Cape land, being 18 feet at high water in the shallowest place in the channel, just at the entrance, but that as soon as this shallow place is passed, a half cable length inward, thirty and thirty-five feet water is found, which continues that depth for twenty-one miles, when the river becomes shallower until there is only twenty-feet depth running down to ten feet (where Wilmington now stands).

These bold voyagers brought their vessel some distance higher than Wilmington, and were much pleased with the land on the main river above Point Petre.

They found many Indians living on their plantations of corn, which were also well stocked with fat cattle and hogs stolen from the Massachusetts settlers of 1660 on the Cape opposite Orton Point. Game was very abundant, and fish was also plentiful. During an expedition higher up in a small boat, they killed four swan, ten geese, ten turkeys, forty ducks, thirty-six paraquitos and seventy plover.

They were attacked by Indians once; a display of fire-arms afterwards compelled the peaceful recognition of the natives. And when the ship reached Crane Island (now Big Island) on the return, Sunday, 29th November, 1663, they met the first ruler of the "Cape Fear Country," the Indian Chief Watcoosa, who sold the river and land to the Barbadians, Anthony Long, William Hilton and Peter Fabian.

A ludicrous incident which the virtuous Barbadians took very seriously occurred during their negotiations. The King, Watcoosa, accompanied by forty lusty warriors, made a long speech to them, which, although unintelligible to the white men, was undoubtedly of a peaceful nature, as he indicated by pantomime that he would cut off the heads of any of his people who attempted to injure them, and in testimony of his goodwill, at the conclusion of his discourse he presented to the Barbadian Captain two very handsome and proper young Indian women, whom the voyagers were given to understand were the King's daughters. These guileless maidens of the Cape Fear, whom Hilton describes as the tallest and most beautiful women he ever saw, were not at all shy, but forced their way into the white men's boat and refused to leave it. Captain Hilton probably had a wife at home, and the thought of presenting these two beautiful girls in their native costume to his better half in Barbadoes must have appalled the stout-hearted explorer who had already faced so many lesser dangers. He loaded them with presents; he gallantly entreated them to call again, but they laughingly shook their heads, and pointing to the ship, indicated their purpose to remain with him for better for worse. What was the poor man to do? Worse still, thought the Captain, what will Mrs. Hilton do! He met the emergency as little George Washington did *not* do. He presented to the father a little hatchet, and he told him a lie. He promised to take the girls aboard in four days; but, alas! their names do not appear later in the passenger-list for the homeward voyage. It is said that for many years after, these disappointed maidens might be seen on the Cape lands shading their eyes as they gazed towards the Southern horizon, looking in vain for the return of the perfidious Hilton, who wisely remained at home when the colonists came to settle on Old Town Creek.

Cushing's Exploits.

Opposite Big Island, on the East side, is Todd's Creek, known as also Mott's Creek, which was the scene of Lieut. William B. Cushing's brave exploit June 23d, 1864. This gallant young naval officer perhaps accomplished more by personal valor than any other individual on either side during the war.

At half-past seven o'clock on the night of May 6th, 1864, the Confederate iron-clad "Raleigh," which was built at the foot of Church street, in Wilmington, proceeded down the river in company with several other smaller boats composing the puny fleet of Commodore Lynch, and under the command of Lieut. J. Pembroke Jones, C. S. N., crossed the New Inlet bar and attacked the blockading fleet. The Federals were taken by surprise, and after a feeble resistance took flight, the "Raleigh" having damaged one or two of the blockaders by her well-directed fire. The Ram was too unwieldy for service at sea, however, and on the second day out Commodore Lynch ordered her back to the river. After crossing the Inlet she stuck on the Rip Shoal and sunk, where she still remains buried in the sand. Lieut. Cushing, then attached to one of the blockaders, the United States steamer "Monticello," with his usual zeal and fearlessness, volunteered to attempt the destruction of the "Raleigh," whose fate was unknown to the Federals. He also undertook a reconnoissance of the defences of the Cape Fear River for the information of the United States Government, which was then preparing an expedition for the capture of Wilmington. Notwithstanding the warning of his superiors that he was almost certain to be captured or killed in this adventure, he persisted in his scheme, and on the night of June 23d, 1864, left his vessel in the first cutter, accompanied by two subordinate officers and fifteen men, crossed the western bar and passed the forts and town of Smithville without discovery, but was very nearly run down by an outward-bound blockade-runner. He then proceeded fearlessly up the river, and with muffled oars steered his boat immediately under the guns of Fort Anderson.

As Cushing attempted to leave Fort Anderson the moon came out from the clouds and disclosed the party to the sentinels, who hailed and immediately opened fire. The fort was roused and the confusion general. Cushing boldly pulled for the opposite banks and swiftly disappeared along the other shore.

His next stopping-place was in this creek, up which he poled his boat until he came to the military road leading from Wilmington to Fort Fisher. Here he cut the telegraph wire and captured a courier from General Whiting with despatches for Colonel Lamb at Fort Fisher. He then put one of his officers (Howorth) in the Confederate's uniform and dispatched him in broad daylight to Wilmington for supplies.

Howorth returned a few hours after with a liberal supply of chickens, eggs and butter, which he had bought without attracting any suspicion. Cushing then waited for darkness, and it is said went in person and also in the courier's clothes to Wilmington, and proceeded to his aunt's house, corner of Eighth and Market streets, where he peeped through the window-blinds and recognized his Confederate kinsfolk, who were of course not made aware of his presence.

On the following day he made sketches of the fortifications around Wilmington and captured a boat-load of Confederates, from whom he learned the fate of the

"Raleigh," which he subsequently inspected in person. He next put his prisoners (six men) into a boat without oars or sails and sent them adrift to get home as best they could. Proceeding down the river, he carefully inspected the torpedo obstructions, and attempted the capture of the Confederate guard-boat near New Inlet. Here he met with formidable resistance, four boats having pursued him, and he was obliged to dash into the breakers on Carolina shoals to escape a large force of Confederates. He reached the blockading squadron safely after an absence of two days and three nights.

His subsequent destruction of the Confederate Ram "Albemarle" is doubtless one of the bravest examples of personal valour in military history.

Cushing's Daring Visit to Fort Anderson.

At early dawn on Friday, February 17th, 1865, the Federal fleet in the river began to bombard Fort Anderson, while the troops under General Schofield attacked the land force and the lines extending westward. The bombardment was kept up all day long with great fury, but the firing ceased at sundown.

About eight o'clock that night the "Eutaw Band," attached to the 25th S. C. Regiment (Colonel C. H. Simonton commanding) came into the Fort and gave a serenade complimentary to the commanding officer (Colonel John J. Hedrick, 40th N. C. Regiment) and his officers. Colonel John D. Taylor was requested by Colonel Hedrick to return thanks to the band, and while he was doing so in a neat and appropriate speech, the officer of the day reported that a boat had been seen passing the Fort and going into the cove on the North side of the Fort. Soon after the speaking the boat was seen pulling out into the river. Captain E. S. Martin had seen the boat going up the river and ordered that the heavy shot be withdrawn from several guns and grape-shot substituted; and when the boat was seen going down the river he ordered the guns fired at it. The boat responded with small arms, and the crew escaped and notified those in the Fort of their safe arrival at the fleet by a single rocket that shot up into the air, and the Confederates heard nothing more of it at that time.

On the 9th or 10th of March, 1865, the same troops which were in the Fort the night above mentioned were at Kinston, N. C., resisting the advance of General Cox's command from New Berne to Goldsboro. The advance guard of General Cox was captured and one of the prisoners gave a Confederate officer a copy of the "New York Herald," which contained an account of a visit made by Captain Cushing to Fort Anderson. He stated that he commanded the boat above mentioned, and had passed into the cove above the Fort, landed and gone into the Fort while Colonel Taylor was speaking. He had hidden himself under one of the guns (which was not in use) on the opposite side of the Fort, about 75 or 100 feet from the speaker, and heard the rest of his speech, which was reported in the account of this visit. The officer (Captain Martin) into whose hands the "Herald" came, having heard the speech of Colonel Taylor, recognized the report as accurate in every particular.

The account also described the escape of Captain Cushing from the Fort and of the boat from the fire of the Confederate guns, and his safe return to his vessel below the Fort.

Carolina Beach.

THE next point of interest on the East side is the wharf of the New Hanover Transit Company, from which there is a short railroad connection of about two miles to the favorite seaside resort, Carolina Beach.

This place was long known to a few of our people as the finest and safest beach on the Atlantic coast, but generation after generation of our inhabitants lived and died without having seen the beautiful foaming breakers curling over these hard white sands, which extend for five miles along this exquisite shore. Before the Wilmington and Wrightsville turnpike was thought of, and long years prior to the building of the Seacoast Railroad, Captain Harper undertook to bring in the steam yacht "Passport" thousands of excursionists from Wilmington and the interior to the health-giving breakers at such a trifling expense, that the humblest and poorest might enjoy the pleasures of surf-bathing, which had hitherto been the exclusive privilege of the rich, until the number has increased to forty and fifty thousand passengers annually.

The steamer "Wilmington" makes four or five trips daily, and the run occupies one hour from Wilmington to the beach.

Gander Hall.

NEAR this landing may be seen a fine grove of old oaks which many years ago sheltered an attractive estate, still known as Gander Hall. It was owned in the year 1830 by Captain James McIlhenny, of an honored and respected family on the Cape Fear. Captain McIlhenny was the victim of a well-known joke which gave the place its peculiar name. An extraordinary trade demand for goose-feathers at high prices led him to purchase in the up country a flock of geese which he intended to use for breeding purposes. He counted the increase before it was hatched, and anticipated with satisfaction large profits from the sale of feathers. The Captain selected the geese in person, and as he wanted white feathers, was careful to accept only the white birds. After waiting an intolerable time for the laying season to begin, he consulted a goose expert, and was informed, to his amazement, that his geese were all ganders.

Sedgeley Abbey.

Near Gander Hall are the ruins of "Sedgeley Abbey," which was the grandest colonial residence of the Cape Fear. It was of about the dimensions and appearance of the Governor Dudley mansion in Wilmington, and was erected about 170 years ago by an English gentleman of wealth and refinement, named Maxwell, who owned all the land as far as Smith's Island. The house was built of coquina, a rock made up of fragments of marine shells slightly consolidated by natural pressure and infiltrated calcareous matter, of which there are still large formations there. The cellar alone remains, having been cut out of the solid rock. The South wing of the building was standing until about 25 years ago, when it was demolished and the material burned for fertilizers by an unsentimental tenant, who might have gathered all the oyster-shells he desired which had been left by the Indians at a slightly greater distance. A beautiful avenue of oaks extended from the mansion on the East for 1,500 feet towards the ocean in full view, and a corduroy road, which may still be seen, was built through a bay and lined with trees to the river landing. Some weird traditions about the house and its lonely master have come down through the neighborhood negroes, who still regard the place with superstitious awe. It is said that several attempts were made many years ago to find some gold alleged to be buried there, and although the times chosen were on bright, clear days, the sky became suddenly overcast, the wind moaned through the roofless walls, and cries and groans were distinctly heard by the treasure-hunters, who did not tarry for further investigation.

First White Settlement.

A FEW miles below this interesting ruin may yet be seen indications of the first white settlement on the Cape Fear in 1661 by the enterprising New Englanders from Massachusetts, who might have prospered, but their greed led them to destruction. For a time they carried on a profitable and apparently peaceable intercourse with the native Indians, but when they sent Indian children North to be sold into slavery under the pretense of instructing them in learning and in the principles of the Christian religion, the red men were not slow to discern their treachery, and from that time, as Lawson says, "they never gave over till they had entirely rid themselves of the English by their bows and arrows."

The New Englanders left much cattle behind them, which the Barbadians four years later found in the possession of the Indians along the Cape Fear.

On this first attempt at a settlement on the Cape Fear river, Bryant, in his "Popular History of the United States," page 272, says: "There were probably few bays or rivers along the coast, from the Bay of Fundy to Florida, unexplored by the New Englanders where there was any promise of profitable trade with the Indians. The colonist followed the trader wherever unclaimed lands were open to occupation. These energetic pioneers explored the sounds and rivers South of Virginia in pursuit of Indian traffic, contrasted the salubrity of the climate and the fertility of the soil with that region of rocks where they had made their homes, and where winter reigns for more than half the year. In 1660 or 1661, a company of these men purchased of the natives and settled upon a tract of land at the mouth of the Cape Fear river. Their first purpose was apparently the raising of stock, as the country seemed peculiarly fitted to grazing, and they brought a number of neat cattle and swine to be allowed to feed at large under the care of herdsmen. But they aimed at something more than this nomadic occupation, and a company was formed, in which a number of adventurers in London were enlisted, to found a permanent colony. Discouraged, however, either by the want of immediate success, or for want of time to carry out their plans, or for some less creditable reason, the settlement was soon abandoned."

Cape Fear Indians.

It is an interesting fact that the descendants of these Indians live in the same locality to the present day, and illustrate an unusual condition—an amalgamation of white, black and Indian races. The Indian characteristics, however, predominate. The men are thrifty, industrious and peaceable; engaged principally in fishing during the shad season, and in cattle-raising upon the same range that was occupied two hundred years ago by their savage ancestors.

Large mounds of oyster-shells, many pieces of broken wicker pottery, arrow-heads, and other relics of the red men are still found on the peninsula below Carolina Beach. During the late war these remains of an Indian settlement were frequently unearthed by the Confederates engaged upon the intrenchments around Fort Fisher; and here are buried the last of the Corees, Cheraws and other small tribes occupying the land once inhabited by the powerful Hatteras Indians. They were allies of the Tuscaroras in 1711, and in an attack upon the English suffered defeat, and have now disappeared from the earth and their dialect is also forgotten. The Hatteras tribe numbered about 3,000 warriors when Raleigh's expedition landed on Roanoke Island in 1584, and when the English made permanent settlements in that vicinity eighty years later, they were reduced to about fifteen bowmen. The Cape Fear Coree Indians told the English settlers of the Yeamans colony in 1669 that their lost kindred of the Roanoke colony, including Virginia Dare, the first white child born in America, had been adopted by the once powerful Hatteras tribe and had become amalgamated with the children of the wilderness. It is believed that the Croatans of this vicinity are descendants of that race.

The Massachusetts settlers referred to the Cape Fear as the Charles river, which was applied, as was also the original name, Carolina, in honor of King Charles IX., of France, during whose reign Admiral Coligny made some settlements of French Huguenots on the Florida coast, and built a fort which he called Charles Fort, on what is now the South Carolina coast.

Lilliput.

NEARLY opposite, surrounded by noble oaks, are the ancient estates of Lilliput and Kendal.

The first record extant of Lilliput plantation is in a patent from the Lords Proprietors, 6th November, 1725, recorded in the Secretary's office of North Carolina, to

Eleazar Allen. Mr. Allen was born at or near Charleston about 1692. He married Sarah, eldest daughter of Colonel William Rhett, about the year 1722. In 1730 he was recommended for one of the council of North Carolina by Governor Burrington, and appointed to that office by the Crown; but he does not appear to have assumed the duties until the 22d of November, 1735. He was appointed in that year with Nathaniel Rice, Roger Moore and Capt. James Innes, a Commissioner to fix the boundary line between North and South Carolina. He was made Receiver General of the Province of North Carolina from 1735 to 1748. During that time he experienced, in common with all the other public treasurers, great difficulty in collecting the quit rents due the Crown, for which he was held personally responsible by the British Government, and for the security of which he ultimately pledged his entire estate, including Lilliput.

An English gentleman who visited the Cape Fear in 1734 with thirteen other travellers, made special mention of Mr. Allen's residence, a beautiful brick house on Lilliput, adjoining Kendal, and also of his well-known hospitality. He says Mr. Allen was then speaker to the Commons, House of Assembly in the Province of South Carolina. Mr. Allen must have lived sumptuously and entertained lavishly, as among the items of personal property in his estate made known at his death, was twelve dozen cut-glass table basins, now known as finger-bowls.

On the death of Mr. Allen, 17th January, 1749, aged fifty-seven years, at Lilliput, where he was buried, this plantation became the property and residence for a time of Sir Thomas Frankland. It was subsequently sold to John Davis, Jr., in 1765.

Sir Thomas Frankland was a grandson of Frances, daughter of Oliver Cromwell, who, upon the death of his brother, Sir Charles Frankland, in 1765, succeeded him as baronet. Sir Thomas was previous to that time an Admiral of the White in the British Navy, a post of great distinction. He married Susan, daughter of William Rhett, Jr., of Charleston. They have numerous descendants now living in England.

We find that, in 1789, Lilliput was in possession of the well-known McRee family of this section, and here was born the distinguished medical practitioner and diagnostician, Dr. James Fergus McRee, who afterwards lived and died in Wilmington.

Kendal.

The adjoining plantation of Kendal was originally owned by "King" Roger Moore, who bequeathed it 7th March, 1747, to his son, George Moore. "King" Roger also devised to other heirs two hundred and fifty negro slaves.

George Moore, of Moore Fields, as he was afterwards called, was remarkable for his great energy, good management and considerable wealth. The original proprietors of the Cape Fear plantations were men of extraordinary discernment and discretion. They first took up all the best land within easy access, laid out and built their plantation residence, and then provided themselves with a comfortable summer house on the Sound. Evidences of this method are still to be seen in the many Sound roads which converge into the old thoroughfare at the east landing of the Brunswick ferry near Big Sugar Loaf and opposite the site of old Brunswick. George Moore's summer place was a tract on the north side of the creek at Masonboro, now owned by the McKoy family. He was twice married, and his wives, with remarkable fidelity and amazing fortitude, presented him every Spring with a new baby, until the number reached twenty-eight. An interesting relic of this extraordinary family is preserved by Mr. Junius Davis. It is a book of Common Prayer, on the fly-leaf of which is inscribed the names and dates of birth of the entire family of twenty-eight children.

In common with the titled class in England, the Cape Fear planters held trade and trades-people in abhorrence, and kept themselves aloof from the commercial centres. They preferred to live on their plantations, and their social life betrayed a class distinction not at all in keeping with the democratic ideas of their descendants. In one respect, however, they greatly differed from the aristocracy of the Old Country—a generous and refined hospitality being universal and proverbial, and this excellent trait is still a striking characteristic of their successors on the river to the present day.

For personal reasons, to avoid the public parade of his numerous family through the town of Wilmington, it suited George Moore to cut a private road for his own use, from his plantation on Rocky Point to Masonboro Sound, by which his faithful wife and her remarkable progeny travelled on horseback in their yearly journeys from the country plantations to the seashore.

Mr. Moore's method of transporting his household effects was unique, by which he employed the services of a large retinue of negro slaves; upon the head of one was placed a table ; upon another a mattress ; a third a chair, and so on, until fifty or more bearers were in line, when the cavalcade proceeded on foot towards Masonboro—an extraordinary and moving spectacle.

When corn was wanted at the summer place, one hundred negro fellows would be started, each with a bushel bag on his head. There is, said the late Dr. John H. Hill, quite a deep ditch leading from some large bay swamps lying to the west of the George Moore road. It used to be called the Devil's Ditch, and there was some mystery and idle tradition as to why and how the ditch was cut there. It was doubtless made to drain the water from those bays, to flood some lands cultivated in rice, which were too low to be drained for corn.

Kendal and Lilliput have been owned and cultivated for years past by Mr. Fred. Kidder, a type of the Old School gentleman, one of the most prominent and industrious planters on the river, a worthy and honored successor of the distinguished settlers on the Cape Fear, described as gentlemen of birth and education, bred in the refinement of polished society, and bringing with them ample fortunes, gentle manners and cultivated minds.

(Orton Plantation.)

Orton.

AMONG the venerable relics of Colonial days in North Carolina there is probably none richer in legendary lore, nor more worthy of historic distinction, than the old Colonial plantation of Orton on the Cape Fear. The name is doubtless taken from the old town or village of Orton, near Kendal, in the beautiful lake district of England, from whence the ancestors of the Moore family on the Yeamans side may have come to Barbadoes; the line of the Moore family being of Scotch Irish origin, as there is a Kendal Point and it is said an Orton plantation on that Island, which was the home of Sir John Yeamans, who afterwards settled upon the Cape Fear and was Governor of Clarendon.

Orton plantation was owned originally by Maurice Moore, the grandson of Governor Sir John Yeamans, and the son of Governor James Moore, of South Carolina, who came with his brother, Colonel James Moore, to suppress the Tuscarora Indian outbreaks in the Province of North Carolina in 1711. From him it passed to his brother, Roger Moore, known ever afterwards as "King" Roger. He was a man of lordly and distinguished bearing, and owned immense bodies of land in this part of the country, and was for many years a member of Governor Gabriel Johnston's Council. During his absence from home, in the early days of the settlement, his house at Orton was attacked, pillaged and burned by the Cree Indians, who lived on the Cape opposite the plantation. Some days afterwards "King" Roger, with a small force of neighbors and servants, seeing the Indians at play and bathing in the river near Big Sugar Loaf, marched up the river out of sight, crossed over, and taking the savages by surprise, exterminated the whole tribe. His tomb, a brick mound, is still in a good state of preservation in the old family burying-ground at Orton. The spot, which has unfortunately in recent years been partly cleared, is described by the author of "Roanoke" as follows:

"I found myself in one of those spots which nature herself seems to have consecrated for her most holy rites. There was not a shrub, nor a blade of grass, within this sacred temple; there the garish beams of the sun never penetrate, but even at noonday a deep, solemn twilight reigns. The oaks, whose multitudinous branches form a thick canopy above us, looked as if they had witnessed the flight of centuries; and from their limbs and trunks there streamed hoary and luxuriant flakes of moss sweeping almost to the ground, and looking like elfin locks whitened by the frosts of a thousand years. Within this druid temple there are old brick vaults, without a name and without a date; and here, because, perhaps, nature herself seems to have formed a cemetery for her favorite child—here, beneath one of these vaults and close by the banks of the old Cape Fear, are supposed to repose the ashes of Utopia. The scene and the recollections which it awakened threw me into a meditative mood, and seating myself on one of the vaults, and looking out on the broad but lovely expanse of waters before me, I remained, listening to the subdued murmur of the distant ocean."

This fine property was sold about the year 1860, with the slaves upon it, for one hundred thousand dollars; but the purchase money was never paid, and the estate deteriorated for more than fifteen years from inattention and decay. In 1876, a young English gentleman of education and refinement, named Currer Richardson

Roundel (a nephew of Sir Roundel Palmer who afterwards became Lord Chancellor of Great Britain as Lord Selborne), came to Wilmington evidently suffering with some mental disorder. He was induced by the agents to buy Orton, which had been in the market for some time previous, and he undertook to reclaim it, but met with difficulties which he had not anticipated, and which so depressed him that he took his own life. The writer found him early on the morning of July 26th, 1876, in his room at the hotel in Wilmington stripped to the waist, and lying upon the floor in a pool of blood, the deadly pistol in one hand, the other hand pointing to a ragged hole in his forehead. He was dead. He was buried by kind and gentle hands in Oakdale near Wilmington.

The present beautiful residence, with its majestic columns and its white and glittering vestments, now occupied by Colonel K. M. Murchison, the proprietor, was built about the year 1725 by "King" Roger Moore, of brick brought from England, and was afterwards enlarged and improved by the late Dr. Fred. J. Hill, a rice-planter, an intelligent gentleman, and a princely citizen, who was noted far and near for his elegant and refined hospitality.

Colonel Murchison has brought the plantation up to its best production—about a hundred laborers are employed and many expensive permanent improvements have been adopted. He resides here with his family during the winter months, his home and principal business being in New York City.

These ten thousand acres include a fine game preserve, which is greatly enjoyed by the Colonel and his friends, to whom the pleasures of the chase are its principal attraction.

Born and reared on the upper Cape Fear of Scotch ancestors whose brain and brawn have ever infused new life and vigor throughout the business world, Colonel K. M. Murchison is honored; for out of nothing but a stout heart, an honest purpose and a good name, he has built up a fortune and achieved a reputation for integrity and usefulness among men who only acknowledge such as leaders.

He deserves well of Wilmington because he has given liberally of his means for the development of our trade and industries. When there was not a hotel in the place worthy of the name, and when it was said that this lack barred a class of visitors hitherto unknown, but greatly to be desired by the community, he came forward and fearlessly invested a large amount in a first-class hotel, of which we should all be proud, although it has not been properly appreciated. Were our citizens animated with a little of the public spirit of their forefathers, who gave three hundred and fifty thousand dollars to build and equip a Wilmington railroad, when the entire taxables were only three hundred thousand dollars, "The Orton" would always be filled to overflowing and such an enterprise receive its just reward.

Colonel Murchison served throughout the war as Colonel of the 54th N. C. Troops, took part in the active Virginia campaigns, and upon the conclusion of peace returned to New York, where he has ever since been engaged in business.

(Colonial Governor's Palace.)

Colonial Governor Tryon's Palace— Scene of the First Outbreak of the Revolutionary War.

About half a mile to the South of Orton House, and within the boundary of the plantation, are the ruins of Governor Tryon's residence, memorable in the history of the United States as the spot upon which the first overt act of violence occurred in the war of American Independence, and nearly eight years before the Boston

Tea incident, of which so much has been made in Northern history; while this Colonial ruin, the veritable cradle of American liberty, is probably unknown to nine-tenths of the people on the Cape Fear at the present day.

This place, which has been eloquently referred to by two of the most distinguished sons of the Cape Fear, and direct descendants of Sir John Yeamans, the late Hon. George Davis and the Hon. A. M. Waddell, and which was known as Russelborough, was bought from William Moore, son and successor of "King" Roger, by Captain John Russell, Commander of His Britannic Majesty's sloop of war "Scorpion," who gave the tract of about fifty-five acres his own name. It subsequently passed into the possession of his widow, who made a deed of trust, and the property ultimately again became a part of Orton plantation. It was sold March 31st, 1758, by the executors of the estate of William Moore to the British Governor and Commander-in-Chief, Arthur Dobbs, who occupied it and who sold it or gave it to his son, Edward Bryce Dobbs, Captain in His Majesty's 7th Regiment of Foot or Royal Fusileers, who conveyed it by deed dated February 12th, 1767, to His Excellency William Tryon, Governor, etc. It appears, however, tnat Governor Tryon occupied this residence prior to the date of this deed, as is shown by the following official correspondence in 1766 with reference to the uprising of the Cape Fear people in opposition to the Stamp Act:

"BRUNSWICK, 19th FEBRUARY, 1766,
"ELEVEN AT NIGHT.

"SIR:—

"Between the hours of six and seven o'clock this evening, Mr. Geo. Moore and Mr. Cornelius Harnett waited on me at my house, and delivered to me a letter signed by three gentlemen. The inclosed is a copy of the original. I told Mr. Moore and Mr. Harnett that as I had no fears or apprehensions for my person or property, I wanted no guard, therefore desired the gentlemen might not come to give their protection where it was not necessary or required, and that I would send the gentlemen an answer in writing to-morrow morning. Mr. Moore and Mr. Harnett might stay about five or six minutes in my house. Instantly after their leaving me, I found my house surrounded with armed men to the number I estimate at one hundred and fifty. I had some altercation with some of the gentlemen, who informed me their business was to see Capt. Lobb, whom they were informed was at my house; Captain Paine then desired me to give my word and honor whether Captain Lobb was in my house or not. I positively refused to make any such declaration, but as they had force in their hands I said they might break open my locks and force my doors. This, they declared, they had no intention of doing; just after this and other discourse, they got intelligence that Captain Lobb was not in my house. The majority of the men in arms then went to the town of Brunswick, and left a number of men to watch the avenues of my house, therefore think it doubtful if I can get this letter safely conveyed. I esteem it my duty, sir, to inform you, as Fort Johnston has but one officer, and five men in garrison, the Fort will stand in need of all the assistance the "Viper" and "Diligence" sloops can give the commanding officer there, should any insult be offered to his Majesty's fort or stores, in which case it is my duty to request of you to repel force with force, and take on board his Majesty's sloops so much of his Majesty's ordnance, stores and ammunition out of the said fort as you shall think necessary for the benefit of the service.

"I am, sir, your most humble servant,

(Signed) "WM. TRYON."

"To the Commanding Officer, either of the Viper or Diligence Sloops of War."

The writer, who frequently enjoys the old-time hospitality of Orton, had often inquired for the precise location of the ruins of Governor Tryon's Russelborough residence, without success. But during a recent visit, and acting upon Colonel Waddell's reference to its site on the north of old Brunswick, the service of an aged negro who had lived continuously on the plantation for over seventy years was engaged, who, being questioned, could not remember ever having heard the name Russelborough, nor of Governor Dobbs, nor of Governor Tryon, nor of an avenue of trees in the locality described. He said he remembered, however, hearing when he was a boy about a man named "Governor Palace," who had lived in a great house between Orton and old Brunswick.

We proceeded at once to the spot, which is approached through an old field, still known as the Old Palace Field, on the other side of which, on a bluff facing the east, and affording a fine view of the river, we found hidden in a dense undergrowth of timber the foundation walls of Tryon's residence. The aged guide showed us the well worn carriage road of the Governor, and also his private path through the old garden to the river landing, a short distance below, on the south of which is a beautiful cove of white and shining sand, known, he said, in olden times, as the Governor's Cove. The stone foundation walls of the house are about two feet above the surface of the ground. Some sixty years ago the walls stood about twelve to fifteen feet high, but the material was unfortunately used by one of the proprietors for building purposes.

The old servant pointed out a large pine tree near by, upon which he said had been carved in Colonial times the names of two distinguished persons buried beneath it, and which in his youthful days was regarded with much curiosity by visitors. The rude inscription has unhappily become almost obliterated by several growths of bark, and the strange, mysterious record is forever hidden by the hand of time.

A careful excavation of this ruin would doubtless reveal some interesting and possibly valuable relics of Governor Tryon's household. Near the surface was found, while these lines were being written, some fragments of blue Dutch tiling, doubtless a part of the interior decorations; also a number of peculiarly shaped bottles for the favorite sack of those days, which Falstaff called Sherris sack, of Xeres vintage, now known as dry sherry.

Ruins of Brunswick.

About a quarter of a mile distant towards the South, and yet within the limits of this time-honored estate of Orton, are the ruins of the old Colonial town of Brunswick, once the chief seaport and seat of government of the Province of North Carolina. Its public buildings and substantial houses have long ago crumbled to their foundations, which still remain.

The daily hum of traffic has long since ceased, and the busy feet that trod its now silent streets have mouldered into dust.

> "No more for them the blazing hearth shall burn,
> Nor busy housewife ply her evening care,
> Nor children run to greet their sire's return,
> Or climb his knee the envied kiss to share."

The glad voices of the village children, the merry ring of the blacksmith's anvil and the hearty yo-ho of the sailors in the bay have melted away into the silence of the dead, which is only broken by the hooting owl and the barking fox, or by the plaintive cry of the whippoorwill and the plunge of the osprey in the now peaceful waters of the Governor's Cove, while from across the narrow isthmus is heard the moaning of the lonely sea.

Ruins of St. Philip's Church.

WITHIN the boundaries of this forgotten town are the picturesque ruins of St. Philip's Church, which was built by the citizens of Brunswick and principally by the landed gentry about the year 1740. In the year 1751 Mr. Lewis Henry DeRosset, a member of Governor Gabriel Johnston's Council and subsequently an expatriated Royalist, introduced a bill appropriating to the church of St. Philip at Brunswick and to St. James' Church at Wilmington, equally, a fund that was realized by the capture and destruction of a pirate vessel, which, with a squadron of Spanish privateers, had entered the river and plundered the plantations. A picture ("ECCE HOMO"), captured from this pirate, is still preserved in the vestry-room of St. James' Church in Wilmington.

St. Philip's Church was built of large brick brought from England. Its walls are nearly three feet thick and are solid and almost intact still, the roof and the floor only having disappeared. Its dimensions are nearly as large as those of our modern churches, being 76 feet 6 inches long, 53 feet 3 inches wide, standing walls 24 feet 4 inches high. There are 11 windows, measuring 15x7 feet, and 3 large doors. It must have possessed much architectural beauty and massive grandeur with its high pitched roof, its lofty doors and beautiful chancel windows.

Upon the fall of Fort Fisher, which is a few miles to the southeast of Orton, in 1865, the Federal troops visited the ruins of St. Philip's, and with pick-axes dug out the corner-stone, which had remained undisturbed for one hundred and twenty-five years, and which doubtless contained papers of great interest and value to our people. It is a singular fact that during the terrific bombardment of Fort Anderson, which was erected on Orton, and which enclosed with earthworks the ruins of St. Philip's, while many of the tombs in the church-yard were shattered and broken to pieces by the storm of shot and shell, the walls escaped destruction; as if the Power Above had shielded from annihilation the building which had been dedicated to His service.

This sanctuary has long been a neglected ruin, trees of a larger growth than the surrounding forest have grown up within its roofless walls, and where long years ago the earnest prayer and song of praise ascended up on high, a solemn stillness reigns, unbroken save by the distant murmur of the sea, which ever sings a requiem to the buried past.

In concluding his most interesting sketch of old

Brunswick, in "A Colonial Officer and His Times," the graceful and gifted author, Colonel Alfred Moore Waddell, says:

"Memorable for some of the most dramatic scenes in the early history of North Carolina as the region around Brunswick was (being the theatre of the first open armed resistance to the Stamp Act, and not far from the spot where the first victory of the Revolution crowned the American arms at Moore's Creek Bridge, on the 27th of February, 1776), its historic interest was perpetuated when, nearly a century afterwards, its tall pines trembled and its sand-hills shook to the thunder of the most terrific artillery fire that has ever occurred since the invention of gun-powder, when Fort Fisher was captured in 1865. Since then it has again relapsed into its former state, and the bastions and traverses and parapets of the whilom Fort Anderson are now clad in the same exuberant robe of green with which generous nature in that clime covers every neglected spot. And so the old and the new ruin stand side by side in mute attestation of the utter emptiness of all human ambition; while the Atlantic breeze sings gently amid the sighing pines, and the vines cling more closely to the old church wall, and the lizard basks himself where the sunlight falls on a forgotten grave."

Colonial Ferry and Inn.

THE ruins of an inn and ferry-house attract attention at old Brunswick landing. This ferry to the landing at Big Sugar Loaf on the opposite side of the river, a distance of over two miles, must have been an exposed and dangerous passage during stormy weather. It was kept by Cornelius Harnett and connected with the only road to the northern part of the Province. This Colonial road is still used at the present day, and may be seen at the old landing place near Big Sugar Loaf.

It is interesting to recall the fact as stated by Doctor Brickell, a Dublin gentleman who visited this region in 1737, that the people on the Cape Fear were invariably comfortable and prosperous, and that they were also exceedingly hospitable and kindly. The planters cultivated rice, of which he says there were several sorts—"some bearded, others not so; besides there was the white and red rice, the latter the better." Indian corn was largely produced; fruits were plentiful; game abundant; cattle thrived and fattened in rich pastures; horse-racing, wrestling and foot-racing were favorite amusements. He says the women were well featured, brisk and charming in their conversation and as "finely shaped as any in the world;" that "they marry very young, some at thirteen and fourteen," and that "a spinster of twenty is reckoned a stale maid." The houses were full of healthy children.

Mr. Harnett entertained his patrons at the Inn with a liberal diet of beef, pork, venison, wild and tame fowl, fish of several delicate sorts, "roots" (vegetables, probably), several kinds of salads, good bread, butter, milk, cheese, rice, Indian corn, hasty pudding, rum, brandy, cider, persimmon beer, cedar beer, castena or tanpanan, Indian tea, etc.

Confederate Fortifications.

WE now approach the ruins of Fort Anderson, Battery Hoke, Camp Wyatt (so named for the first victim of the war, private Henry A. Wyatt, of the 1st N. C. Regiment, killed at the battle of Big Bethel), Battery Buchanan, Fort Fisher and Mound Battery, famous as the gateway of the Southern Confederacy, and for months the only key to the outside world from which was replenished its scant supplies of army stores.

It has been well said by a prominent ex-officer of the late C. S. Navy that "the fall of Wilmington was the severest blow to the Confederate cause which it could receive from the loss of any port. It was far more injurious than the capture of Charleston, and but for the moral effect, even more hurtful than the evacuation of Richmond. With Wilmington and the Cape Fear open, the supplies that reached the Confederate armies would have enabled them to maintain an unequal contest for years; but with the fall of Fort Fisher, the constant stream of supplies was effectually cut off and the blockade made truly effective—not by the navy fleet, but by its captures on land."

Fort Anderson.

Fort Anderson and Orton House, the latter used as the headquarters of Captain E. S. Martin, Chief of Ordnance, were the last Confederate positions evacuated upon the river, and they were abandoned to superior force a month after Fort Fisher fell.

At nine o'clock on the evening of Sunday, January 15th, 1865, Fort Fisher, which had for years stubbornly resisted the bombardments and assaults of the Federal fleet and forces, was overcome. On Monday and Monday night, Fort Holmes, on Smith's Island, Forts Caswell and Campbell, on Oak Island, and Fort Pender (Johnston), at Smithville, were evacuated by the Confederates. On Friday of the same week, the garrisons of these forts were assembled at Fort Anderson under command of General Hebert. He was soon relieved in command by General Johnson Hagood, who commanded until Fort Anderson was evacuated.

After the capture of Fort Fisher, the Federals were employed in getting their monitors and gun-boats over the shoals called the Rip, near New Inlet, into the river. This was a tedious process. The heavy guns and turrets were slowly removed to lighten the draft, and these were afterwards replaced for an assault upon Fort Anderson, the last stronghold of the weary, half-starved, but devoted band of Southerners, who calmly awaited their death-blow. The Federal fleet then remained with General Terry's command in and about Fort Fisher in front of General Hoke's line, and made no demonstration until Friday, February 17th, 1865, when General Schofield's corps of 20,000 men having arrived, landed at Fisher, and were transferred to Smithville. Terry then attacked Hoke's line on the east side of the river, and Schofield moved up from Smithville and assaulted Fort Anderson from the rear, while the Federal fleet opened on the Fort from the river.

The bombardment and land attack on Fort Anderson continued all day Friday, Saturday and Saturday night, until Sunday morning, February 19th, about two o'clock, when the Fort was evacuated, and the Confederate troops fell back behind Town Creek, burning the bridges over the creek. Schofield attacked them Sunday and Monday. On Monday afternoon, about four o'clock, the Confederates retreated towards Wilmington, which they entered on Monday night, February 20th, 1865.

Terry and Schofield followed on the 22d and took possession of Wilmington, the Confederates having moved towards North East river during the night of the 21st February.

Sherman, spreading desolation in his track, had already reached Fayetteville and messengers were sent to him by Schofield on board the steam tug J. McB. Davidson, which was the first boat to ascend the Cape Fear after the fall of Wilmington; she was commanded by Captain Marshall, and her Chief Engineer was Mr. Price, both of whom were subsequently lost at sea.

A Colonial Fort.

A SHORT distance below Fort Anderson, on a bluff called Howe's Point, are the remains of a Colonial fort, and behind it the ruins of a residence, in which, tradition says, was born in 1730 one of the greatest heroes of the Revolutionary War (General Robert Howe), the trusted and honored Lieutenant of Washington. He was the son of Job Howe, an educated and wealthy planter on the Cape Fear, who left, in 1748, a plantation to each of his five sons.

It is said that Robert's estate was on Old Town Creek, and that he resided there. It is also stated that he lived for a time at Kendal, and that on the 12th of May, 1776, the British Generals Cornwallis and Clinton landed with a troop of nine hundred men and ravaged General Howe's plantation. Mr. Reynolds, the present intelligent owner and occupant of the Howe place behind the Colonial fort, who took part in building Fort Anderson, says that his father and his grandfather informed him forty years ago that this fort was erected long before the War of the Revolution as a protection against buccaneers and pirates; that his great-grandfather lived with General Howe on this place during the war and took part in a defence of this fort against the British, who drove the Americans out of it; that the latter retreated to Liberty Pond, about a half mile in the rear, pursued by the British; that a stand was made at this pond, the Americans on the west and the enemy on the east side, and that the blood which flowed stained the margin of the beautiful sheet of water which still bears the name of Liberty Pond; and that the Americans again retreated as far as McKenzie's Mill Dam, behind

Kendal, where the British abandoned the pursuit and returned to their ships of war.

Since the foregoing was written, Mr. Reynolds' statement with reference to General Howe's residence has been fully corroborated by the well-known Cape Fear skipper, Captain Sam Price, now eighty-six years old. He remembers distinctly, and has often visited the house known as General Howe's residence, which he says was a large three-story frame building on a stone or brick foundation, on the spot already described just below Old Brunswick, long and still known as Howe's Point.

Fort Fisher.

Colonel William Lamb, who was in command of Fort Fisher, in his admirable report of its defence, says that "the capture of Fort Fisher, N. C., on the 15th of January, 1865, was followed so quickly by the final dissolution of the Southern Confederacy, that the great victory was not fully realized by the American people. The position commanded the last gateway between the Confederate States and the outside world. Its capture, with the resulting loss of all the Cape Fear river defences and of Wilmington, the great importing depot of the South, effectually ended the blockade-running."

General Lee, feeling the importance of the situation, sent word to Colonel Lamb "that Fort Fisher must be held or he could not subsist his army."

Description of Situation.

"The indentation of the Atlantic ocean in the Carolina coast known as Onslow Bay, and the Cape Fear river, running south from Wilmington, form the peninsula known as Federal Point, which during the Civil War was called Confederate Point. Not quite seven miles north of the end of this peninsula stood a high sand-hill

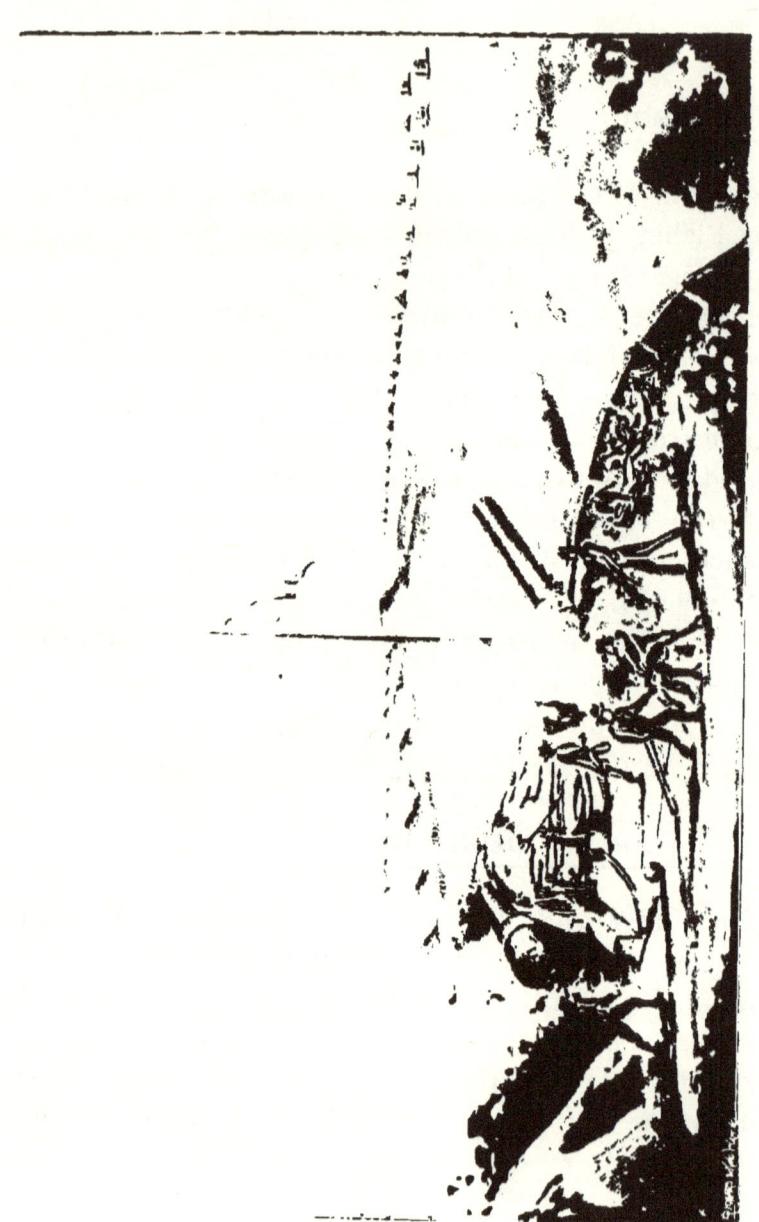

Fort Fisher—Mound Battery.

called the "Sugar Loaf." Here there was an intrenched camp for the army of Wilmington under General Braxton Bragg, the Department Commander, that was hid from the sea by forest and sand-hills. From this intrenched camp the river bank, with a neighboring ridge of sand-dunes, formed a covered way for troops to within a hundred yards of the left salient of Fort Fisher. Between the road and the ocean beach was an arm of Masonboro Sound, and where it ended, three miles north of the fort, were occasional fresh-water swamps, generally wooded with scrub growth, and in many cases quite impassable. Along the ocean shore was an occasional battery formed from a natural sand-hill, behind which Whitworth guns were carried from the fort to cover belated blockade-runners or to protect more unfortunate ones that had been chased ashore.

"About half a mile north of the fort there was a rise in the plain, forming a hill some twenty feet above the tide on the river side, and on this was a redoubt commanding the approach to the fort by the river road. Thus nature, assisted by some slight engineering work, had given a defence to Confederate Point which would have enabled an efficient commander at the intrenched camp, co-operating with the garrison of Fort Fisher, to have rendered the Point untenable for a largely superior force at night when the covering fire of the Federal navy could not distinguish between friend and foe."

The plans of Fort Fisher were Colonel Lamb's, and as the work progressed were approved by Generals French, Raines, Longstreet, Beauregard and Whiting. It was styled by Federal engineers "the Malakoff of the South." It was built solely with the view of resisting the fire of a fleet, and it stood uninjured, except as to armament, two of the fiercest bombardments the world has ever witnessed. The two faces to the works were 2,580 yards long. The land face was 682 yards long, and the sea face 1,898 yards long.

The Land Face of Fort Fisher.

"At the land face of Fort Fisher the peninsula was about half a mile wide. This face commenced about one hundred feet from the river with a half bastion, and extended with a heavy curtain to a full bastion on the ocean side, where it joined the sea face. The work was built to withstand the heaviest artillery fire. There was no moat with scarp and counterscarp, so essential for defense against storming parties, the shifting sands rendering its construction impossible with the material available.

The outer slope was twenty feet high and was sodded with marsh grass, which grew luxuriantly. The parapet was not less than twenty-five feet thick, with an inclination of only one foot. The revetment was five feet nine inches high from the floor of the gun chambers, and these were some twelve feet or more from the interior plane. The guns were all mounted in barbette on Columbiad carriages, there being no casemated gun in the Fort. Between the gun chambers, containing one or two guns each, there were twenty heavy guns on the land face; there were heavy traverses exceeding in size any known to engineers, to protect from an enfilading fire. They extended out some twelve feet or more in height above the parapet, running back thirty feet or more. The gun chambers were reached from the rear by steps. In each traverse was an alternate magazine or bomb-proof, the latter ventilated by an air chamber. The passage ways penetrated traverses in the interior of the work, forming additional bomb-proofs for the reliefs for the guns.

As a defense against infantry, there was a system of sub-terra torpedoes extending across the peninsula, five to six hundred feet from the land-face, and so disconnected that the explosion of one would not affect the others; inside the torpedoes, about fifty feet from the berme of the work, extending from river-bank to sea-shore, was a heavy palisade of sharpened logs nine feet high, pierced for musketry, and so laid out as to have an enfilading fire on the centre, where there was a redoubt guarding a sally-port, from which two Napoleons were run out as occasion required. At the river end of the palisade was a deep and muddy slough, across which was a bridge, the entrance of the river road into the port; commanding this bridge was a Napoleon gun. There were three mortars in the rear of the land face.

The Sea Face of Fort Fisher.

"THE sea face for one hundred yards from the northwest bastion was of the same massive character as the land face. A crescent battery intended for four guns joined this, but it was converted into a hospital bomb-proof. In the rear a heavy curtain was thrown up to protect the chambers from fragments of shells. From the bomb-proof a series of batteries extended for three-quarters of a mile along the sea, connected by an infantry curtain. These batteries had heavy traverses, but were not more than ten or twelve feet high to the top of the parapets, and were built for richochet firing. On the line was a bomb-proof electric battery connected with a system of submarine torpedoes. Farther along, where the channel ran close to the beach, inside the bar, a mound battery sixty feet high was erected, with two heavy guns which had a plunging fire on the channel; this was connected with the battery north of it by a light curtain. Following the line of the works, it was over one mile from the mound to the northeast bastion at the angle of the sea and land faces, and upon this line twenty-four heavy guns were mounted. From the mound for nearly one mile to the end of the Point, was a level sand-plain scarcely three feet above high tide, and much of it was submerged during gales. At the Point was Battery Buchanan, four guns in the shape of an ellipse commanding the Inlet, its two 11-inch guns covering the approach by land. An advanced redoubt with a 24-pounder was added after the attack by the forces on Christmas, 1864. A wharf for large steamers was in close proximity to these works. Battery Buchanan was a citadel to which an over-powered garrison might retreat and with proper transportation be safely carried off at night, and to which re-inforcements could be sent under the cover of darkness."

The Fort Fisher Fight.

GENERAL WHITING, in his official report of the taking of Fort Fisher on the night of the 15th of January, 1865, after an assault of unprecedented fury, both by sea and land, lasting from Friday morning until Sunday night, says:

"On Thursday night the enemy's fleet was reported off the fort. On Friday morning the fleet opened very heavily. On Friday and Saturday, during the furious bombardment of the fort, the enemy was allowed to land without molestation and to throw up a light line of field-works from Battery Ramseur to the river, thus securing his position from molestation and making the fate of Fort Fisher, under the circumstances, but a question of time.

"On Sunday, the fire on the fort reached a pitch of fury to which no language can do justice. It was concentrated on the land face and front. In a short time nearly every gun was dismounted or disabled, and the garrison suffered severely by the fire. At three o'clock the enemy's land force, which had been gradually and slowly advancing, formed in two columns for assault. The garrison, during the fierce bombardment, was not able to stand to the parapets, and many of the re-inforcements were obliged to be kept a great distance from the

BOMBARDMENT OF FORT FISHER.

fort. As the enemy slackened his fire to allow the assault to take place, the men hastily manned the ramparts and gallantly repulsed the right column of assault. A portion of the troops on the left had also repulsed the first rush to the left of the work. The greater portion of the garrison being, however, engaged on the right, and not being able to man the entire work, the enemy succeeded in making a lodgement on the left flank, planting two of his regimental flags in the traverses. From this point we could not dislodge him, though we forced him to take down his flag from the fire of our most distant guns, our own traverses protecting him from such fire. From this time it was a succession of fighting from traverse to traverse and from line to line until nine o'clock at night, when we were overpowered and all resistance ceased.

"The fall both of the General and the Colonel commanding the fort—one about four and the other about four-thirty o'clock, P. M., had a perceptible effect upon the men, and no doubt hastened greatly the result; but we were overpowered, and no skill or gallantry could have saved the place after he effected a lodgement, except attack in the rear. The enemy's loss was very heavy, and so, also, was our own. Of the latter, as a prisoner, I have not been able to ascertain.

"At nine o'clock, P. M., the gallant Major Reilly, who

had fought the fort after the fall of his superiors, reported the enemy in possession of the sally-port. The brave Captain Van Benthuysen, of marines, though himself badly wounded, with a squad of his men, picked up the General and Colonel and endeavored to make way to Battery Buchanan, followed by Reilly with the remnant of the forces. On reaching there, it was found to be evacuated, by whose order and what authority, I know not; no boats were there. The garrison of Fort Fisher had been coolly abandoned to its fate. Thus fell Fort Fisher after three days battle unparalleled in the annals of the war. Nothing was left but to await the approach of the enemy, who took us about 10 P. M. The fleet surpassed its tremendous efforts in the previous attack. The fort has fallen in precisely the manner indicated so often by myself, and to which your attention has been so frequently called, and in the presence of the ample force provided by you to meet the contingency."

Colonel Lamb, in his report, says he had half a mile of land face and one mile of sea face to defend with 1,900 men. He knew every company present and its strength. This number included the killed, wounded and sick.

To capture Fort Fisher, the enemy lost, by their own statement, 1,445 killed, wounded and missing. Nineteen hundred Confederates with 44 guns, contending against

10,000 men on shore and 600 heavy guns afloat, killing and wounding almost as many of the enemy as there were soldiers in the fort, and not surrendering until the last shot was expended.

The garrison consisted of two companies of the 10th North Carolina under Major Reilly; the 36th North Carolina, Colonel William Lamb, ten companies; four companies of the 40th North Carolina; Company D of the 1st North Carolina Artillery Battalion; Company C 3d North Carolina Artillery Batallion; Company D 13th North Carolina Artillery Batallion, and the Naval Detachment under Captain Van Benthuysen.

General Whiting had been assigned to no duty by General Bragg, although it was his right to have commanded the supporting troops. He determined to go to the fort and share its fate. The Commander, Colonel Lamb, offered to relinquish the control, but General Whiting declined to take away the glory of the defense from him, but remained with him and fought as a volunteer. It is related that during the fight, when one hundred immense projectiles were being hurled per minute at the fort, General Whiting was seen "standing with folded arms, smiling upon a 400-pound shell, as it stood smoking and spinning like a billiard-ball on the sand not twenty feet away until it burst, and then moved quietly away." During the fight General Whiting saw the Federal flags planted on the traverses. Calling on the troops to follow him, they fought hand to hand with clubbed muskets, and one traverse was taken. Just as he was climbing the other, and had his hand upon the Federal flag to tear it down, he fell, receiving two wounds. Colonel Lamb, a half-hour later, fell with a desperate wound through the hip. The troops fought on. Lamb, in the hospital, found voice enough, though faint unto death, to say: "I will not surrender"; and Whiting, lying among the surgeons near by, responded: "Lamb, if you die, I will assume command, and I will never surrender."

After the fort was captured and General Whiting was made prisoner, he was taken to Fort Columbus, on Governors' Island, and there died, March 10th, 1865.

The fearless defender of the last stand at Fisher, Major James Reilly, remained not far from the scene of his exploits until his death, November 5th, 1894.

Colonel William Lamb still survives, and since the war has resided continuously at his home in Norfolk, Virginia, where he is engaged in business

Another prominent officer of the Cape Fear, Colonel George Tait, a gallant Scotchman from Bladen county, who volunteered at the outbreak of the war and remained in active service to the end, is also living in

Norfolk. Always beloved and honored as a soldier and a gentleman, he has in his declining years the comforts and respect achieved by an honorable, active and successful business life.

RESIDENCE OF THE COMMANDER OF FORT FISHER

Craig's Landing.

From the deck of the steamer Wilmington the watchful tourist may espy near Craig's Landing a weather-beaten little cottage of very humble aspect. This unpretentious building was the residence of the Commandant of Fort Fisher and his little family during the war. It is worth preserving, because one of the sweetest little flowers of Confederate womanhood graced its rough interior, and encouraged by her noble self-sacrificing spirit the gallant defenders of the Lost Cause. She, too, has crossed over the river, and rests under the shade of the trees. Like a gentle exhalation she has passed away, but the memory of her devoted life of faith and fortitude, her loving and tender sympathy for the sick and wounded, will live as long as the story of Fisher is told.

By the courtesy of our friend who was her worthy husband, we are permitted to copy the following sketch published some months ago in the "Southern Historical Papers" of Richmond:

The Heroine of Confederate Point.

"In the Fall of 1857, a lovely Puritan maiden, still in her teens, was married in Grace Church, Providence, Rhode Island, to a Virginia youth, just passed his majority, who brought her to his home in Norfolk, a typical ancestral homestead, where, beside the 'white folk,' there was quite a colony of family servants, from the pickaninny, just able to crawl, to the old, gray-headed mammy who had nursed "ole Massa." She soon became enamored of her surroundings and charmed with the devotion of her colored maid, whose sole duty it was to wait upon her young missis. When the John Brown raid burst upon the South and her husband was ordered to Harper's Ferry, there was not a more indignant matron in all Virginia, and when at last secession came, the South did not contain a more enthusiastic little rebel.

"On the 15th of May, 1862, a few days after the surrender of Norfolk to the Federals, by her father-in-law, then Mayor, amid the excitement attending a captured city, her son Willie was born. Cut off from her husband and subjected to the privations and annoyances incident to a subjugated community, her father insisted upon her coming with her children to his home in Providence; but, notwithstanding she was in a luxurious home, with all that parental love could do for her, she preferred to leave all these comforts to share with her husband the dangers and privations of the South. She vainly tried to persuade Stanton, Secretary of War, to let her and her three children with a nurse return to the South; finally he consented to let her go by flag of truce from Washington to City Point, but without a nurse, and as she was unable to manage three little ones, she left the youngest with his grandparents, and with two others bravely set out for Dixie. The generous outfit of every description which was prepared for the journey and which was carried to the place of embarkation, was ruthlessly cast aside by the inspectors on the wharf, and no tears or entreaties or offers of reward by the parents availed to pass anything save a scanty supply of clothing and other necessaries. Arriving in the South, the brave young mother refused the proffer of a beautiful home in Wilmington, the occupancy of the grand old mansion at "Orton," on the Cape Fear river, but insisted upon taking up her abode with her children and their colored nurse in the upper room of a pilot's house, where they lived until the soldiers of the garrison built her a cottage one mile north of Fort Fisher on the Atlantic beach. In both of these homes she was occasionally exposed to the shot and shell fired from blockaders at belated blockade-runners.

"It was a quaint abode, constructed in most primitive style, with three rooms around one big chimney, in which North Carolina pine-knots supplied heat and light on winter nights. This cottage became historic and was famed for the frugal but tempting meals which its charming hostess would prepare for her distinguished guests. Besides the many illustrious Confederate Army and Navy officers who were delighted to find this bit of sunshiny civilization on the wild sandy beach, ensconced among the sand-dunes and straggling pines and black-jack, many celebrated English naval officers enjoyed its hospitality under assumed names;

Roberts, afterwards the renowned Hobart Pasha, who commanded the Turkish navy; Murray, now Admiral Aynsley, long since retired, after having been rapidly promoted for gallantry and meritorious services in the British navy; the brave but unfortunate Burgoyne, who went down in the British iron-clad "Captain" in the Bay of Biscay; and the chivalrous Hewitt, who won the Victoria Cross in the Crimea and was knighted for his services as Ambassador to King John of Abyssinia, and who, after commanding the Queen's yacht, died lamented as Admiral Hewitt. Besides these, there were many genial and gallant merchant captains, among them Halpin, who afterwards commanded the "Great Eastern" while laying ocean cables; and famous war correspondents, Hon. Francis C. Lawley, M. P., correspondent of the "London Times," and Frank Vizitelli, of the "London Illustrated News," afterwards murdered in the Soudan. Nor must the handsome and plucky Tom Taylor be forgotten, the purser of the "Banshee" and the "Night Hawk," who, by his coolness and daring, escaped with a boat's crew from the hands of the Federals after capture off the fort, and who was endeared to the children as the "Santa Claus" of the war.

"At first the little Confederate was satisfied with pork and potatoes, corn-bread and rye coffee, with sorghum sweetening, but after the blockade-runners made her acquaintance the impoverished store-room was soon filled to overflowing, notwithstanding her heavy requisitions on it for the post hospital, the sick and wounded soldiers and sailors always being a subject of her tenderest solicitude, and often the hard-worked and poorly-fed colored hands blessed the little lady of the cottage for a tempting treat.

"Full of stirring events were the two years passed in the cottage on Confederate Point. The drowning of Mrs. Rose Greenough, the famous Confederate spy, off Fort Fisher, and the finding of her body, which was tenderly cared for, and the rescue from the waves, half dead, of Professor Holcombe and his restoration, were incidents never to be forgotten. Her fox-hunting with horse and hounds, the narrow escapes of friendly vessels, the fights over blockade-runners driven ashore, the execution of deserters and the loss of an infant son, whose little spirit went out with the tide one sad summer night, all contributed to the reality of this romantic life.

"When Porter's fleet appeared off Fort Fisher, December, 1864, it was storm-bound for several days, and the little family, with their household goods, were sent across the river to "Orton," before Butler's powder-ship blew up. After the Christmas victory over Porter and Butler the little heroine insisted upon coming back to her cottage, although her husband had procured a home of refuge in Cumberland county. General Whiting protested against her running the risk, for on dark nights her husband could not leave the fort; but she said, 'if the firing became too hot, she would run behind the sand-hills as she had done before,' and come she would.

"The fleet re-appeared unexpectedly on the night of the 12th of January, 1865. It was a dark night, and when the lights of the fleet were reported, her husband sent a courier to the cottage to instruct her to pack up quickly and be prepared to leave with children and nurse as soon as he could come to bid them good-bye. The garrison barge with a trusted crew was stationed at Craig's Landing, near the cottage. After midnight, when all necessary orders were given for the coming attack, the Colonel mounted his horse and rode to the cottage, but all was dark and silent. He found the message had been delivered, but his brave wife had been so undisturbed by the news that she had fallen asleep and no preparations for a retreat had been made. Precious hours had been lost, and as the fleet would soon be shelling the beach and her husband have to return to the fort, he hurried them into the boat as soon as dressed, with only what could be gathered up hastily, leaving dresses, toys and household articles to fall into the hands of the foe. Among the articles left was a writing desk, with the following unfinished letter, which after many years has been returned. It is such a touching picture of those old Confederate days that consent has been given to its publication:

"'THE COTTAGE,' JANUARY 9th, 1865.

"MY OWN DEAR PARENTS:

"I know you have been anxious enough about us all, knowing what a terrible bombardment we have had, but I am glad that I can relieve your mind on our behalf and tell you that we are all safe and well, through a most merciful and kind Providence. God was with us from the first, and our trust was so firm in Him that I can truly say that both Will and I 'feared no evil'.

"I staid in my comfortable little home until the fleet appeared, when I packed up and went across the river to a large but empty house, of which I took possession; a terrible gale came on which delayed the attack for several days, but Saturday it came at last in all its fury; I could see it plainly from where I was; I had very powerful glasses, and sat on a stile out doors all day watching it—an awful but magnificent sight.

"I kept up very bravely (*for you know I am brave*, and *would*, if *I thought I could*, whip Porter and Butler myself), until the last gun had ceased and it began to get dark and still. I was overcome at last and laid my head on the fence and cried for the first and last time during it all. I then got my carriage and rode to a fort near by to learn the news, but my heart failed as I approached it, and I returned to the house and waited a dispatch, which I received about 11 o'clock, saying all was well. I was quite touched with a little incident which occurred during the day; the little ones looked very grave and thoughtful; at last Dick came to me in the midst of the roaring and awful thundering and said: 'Mamma, I want to pray to God for my papa'. He knelt down and said his little earnest prayer; then jumped up, exclaiming and dancing about: 'Oh, sister, I am so glad! I am so glad! Now *God* will keep care of my papa'!

"The shelling was even more terrific on Sunday, and I, not knowing how long it might continue, concluded to go to Fayetteville, and started Sunday noon in a small steamer, with the sick and wounded, to Wilmington, where I was obliged to stay for several days in great suspense, not able to get away and not able to hear directly from Will, as the enemy had cut the wires—and then a martyr to all kinds of rumors—one day heard that Will had lost a leg, etc., etc.; but I steadfastly made up my mind to give no credit to anything bad. At last I heard again that we had driven our persecutors off, and I returned again to the place where I went first, and the next day Will came over for me and took me to the fort, which I rode all over on horseback, but we did not move over for nearly a week. The fort was strewn with missiles of all kinds—it seemed a perfect miracle how any escaped—the immense works were literally skinned of their turf, but not injured in the slightest; not a bomb-proof or a magazine—*and there are more than one*—touched: the magazine the enemy thought they had destroyed was only a caisson; the men had very comfortable quarters in the fort—pretty little white-washed houses—but the shells soon set fire to them, making a large fire and dense smoke, but the works are good for dozen of sieges—plenty of everything; particularly plenty of the greatest essential—*brave hearts.* Our beloved General Whiting was present, but gave up the whole command to Will, to whom he now gives, as is due, the whole credit of building and defending his post, and has urged his promotion to Brigadier-General, which will doubtless be received soon, though neither of us really care for it.

"We expect the Armada again, and will give him a *warmer* reception next time. The fort, expecting a longer time of it, was reserving their heaviest fire for nearer quarters. Butler's 'gallant troops' came right under one side of the fort, but our grape and canister soon drove them off, and *not* Porter's shell, which did not happen to be falling that way at that time; they left their traces sufficiently next morning.

"The 'gallant fellow' who stole the horse from the inside of the fort was doubtless so scared he didn't know much *where* he was. The *true* statement of the thing is, that an officer, unauthorized by Will or the General, sent a courier outside the fort with a message to some troops outside, and soon after he left the fort was attacked and killed by a Yankee sharp-shooter hidden under a bridge. The poor body fell and the *horse* was taken, and the flag spoken of, in the same way, was shot from the parapet and blew outside, when it was taken. When any of them see the inside of the fort, they will never live to tell the tale.

"Ah, mother! you all, at home peacefully, do not know the misery of being driven from home by a miserable, cruel enemy! 'Tis a sad sight to see the sick and aged turned out in the cold to seek a shelter. I cannot speak feelingly because of any feeling myself, as God is so good to us, and has so favored us with life, health and means, and my dear, good husband has provided me a comfortable home in the interior, where I can be safe.

"Will has worried so much about you, dear mother, thinking you would be so anxious about us. He often exclaims, when reading some of the lying accounts: 'How that will worry Ma'!

"How is my darling Willie? We do so want to see our boy. I think Will will have to send for him in the Spring. Kiss the dear one dozen of times for his father and mother.

"Though it was a very unpleasant Christmas to me, still the little ones enjoyed theirs. Will had imported a crowd of toys for them, and they are as happy as possible with them.

"I have not heard from my dear home since last August, and you can imagine how very anxious I am to hear, particularly of dear sister Ria. Is she with George? Do write me of all the dear ones I love so much. How I would love to see you all, so much, and home!

"I forgot to tell you of the casualties in the fight. Ours were only three killed; about sixty wounded; they were all.

Butler's Powder Ship.

In the course of his admirable address to 5,000 ex-Union soldiers at Steinway Hall, New York City, on May 3d, 1878, our silver-tongued orator of the Cape Fear, Colonel Alfred M. Waddell, said:

"While it may be difficult to determine in what engagement of the war the severest concentrated fire of small arms occurred, there can be no doubt as to the place where the power of heavy artillery was exhibited in its most terrific form. The bombardment of Fort Fisher was by far the most frightful that has ever happened since the invention of gun-powder. All the testimony taken before the 'Committee on the Conduct of the War' goes to establish this fact; but, in addition to this, and to the universal admission on the Confederate side, there was still stronger evidence which was given in my presence the day after the capture of the fort by a competent and disinterested witness. The siege of Sebastopol is admitted to have been the greatest bombardment in history up to that time. An English officer, however, who had run the blockade, and who was present at Fort Fisher under an assumed name, was giving an account of it after his escape, and, as preliminary to his remarks, said that he had been at Sebastopol and thought there could never be anything like it again. 'But,' said he,' Sebastopol was the merest child's play compared to what I have witnessed in the last two days. It was simply inconceivable and indescribable in its awful grandeur. I had no conception until now of what an artillery fire could be.' You remember, perhaps, that there was no cessation for more than forty-eight hours, and there were, besides the other projectiles, as many as twenty-five 11-inch shells in the air at the same instant throughout the whole time. Fifty thousand shells were expended by the fleet. During the continuance of the fire it would have been impossible for any living thing to remain on the parapets which I the sea for a mile, and when the assaulting column was formed there was, along that whole front, but a single gun remaining, and that could only be fired once before the fort was reached, and that long, desperate hand-to-hand struggle began. A month before this the celebrated powder-ship explosion occurred, which was intended to blow down this solid earthwork, a mile in extent, with forty-feet traverses every few yards. The best incident of this huge joke was related to me by a distinguished officer of the navy several years ago. The night after the explosion of the powder-ship some of our pickets on the beach were captured and carried on board the Admiral's ship. Among them was a very solemn-looking fellow, who sat silently and sadly chewing tobacco. As there was intense curiosity among the officers of the fleet to know the result of the remarkable experiment, one of them asked the solemn-looking 'Reb' if he was in the fort when the powder-ship exploded; to which he replied in the affirmative, but without exhibiting the least interest in the matter; whereupon the officers gathered around him and began to ask questions:

"You say you were inside the fort?"

"Yes; I was thar."

"What was the effect of the explosion?"

"Mighty bad, sir—powerful bad."

"Well, what was it? Did it kill any rebels or throw down any of the works?"

"No, sir; hit didn't do that."

"Well, what did it do? Speak out."

"Why, stranger, hit waked up pretty nigh every man in the fort!"

The Rocks—Closure of New Inlet.

BEGINNING at Battery Buchanan, a long line of heavy masonry, known as the Rocks, will doubtless interest the traveller.

This sea-wall is one of the best planned and most successful engineering feats in the South. In the year 1761, during a heavy storm, the Atlantic ocean broke across the narrow sand beach which divided the sea from the river some seven miles above the mouth, which from that time became known as the New Inlet, and which caused a rapid shoaling of the old channel, there being then two outlets instead of one as formerly.

The Cape Fear river, from its mouth nearly to Wilmington, is properly a tidal estuary of about thirty-eight square miles. The river and its branches drain an area of about eight thousand square miles. The amount of fresh water passing out at the mouth, though large, is insignificant when compared with the tidal flow which alternately fills and empties this great reservoir. The mean fresh water discharge of the river does not exceed 9,000 cubic feet per second, while the tidal flow at the entrance averages about 175,000 cubic feet per second. This is the real force which creates and preserves the channel across the shifting sands of the coast at the mouth of the river. No demonstration is needed to prove the importance of concentrating this force. It is also apparent that such a force would be most efficient in preserving a passage across a bar and shoals which are in a position sheltered from the prevailing winds and heaviest storms of the coast. This we have at the natural mouth of the river, which is wholly sheltered from northerly, northeasterly, and, in a great measure, from easterly winds by its position in the bay, protected by Cape Fear and Frying Pan Shoals.

Congress was accordingly petitioned by our people to appropriate the necessary means for increasing the depth of water on Cape Fear bar and river; and after careful surveys and estimates by the Corps of Engineers U. S. A., it was decided to undertake the entire closure of New Inlet under the direction of Colonel W. P. Craighill. This important and difficult work was begun in 1875. A continuous line of mattresses composed of logs and brushwood sunk and loaded with stone, was laid entirely across the New Inlet from October, 1875, to June, 1876. This was the foundation of the dam. The work was continued from year to year by piling small stone rip-rap on and over this foundation, bringing it up to high water, and then covering it with heavy granite stones on the top and slopes to low water. The closure was completed successfully in 1881 and was the occasion of much rejoicing in Wilmington, for its failure would have completely ruined the port of Wilmington, which depends for its life upon deep water and successful competition with Norfolk and Charleston.

The length of the dam from Federal Point to Zeke's Island is one mile, but the extension of Zeke's Island jetties to Smith's Island makes the line much longer. The Rock foundation of this wall is from 90 feet to 120 feet wide at the base. and for three-fourths of the line the average depth of the stone wall is 30 feet from the top of the dam. In some places it is 36 feet deep. The stone used in this gigantic structure would build a solid wall eight feet high, four feet thick and one hundred miles long. The cost of the work was $480,000—a small sum when the magnitude and difficulty of the undertaking is considered.

Battery Lamb—Confederate Salt Works.

Passing Battery Lamb, a Confederate work on Reeves' Point, we come to Walden's Creek, upon which were established, in war times, large Confederate Salt Works for the supply of this indispensable article to the soldiers of the South.

The salt-water was carried in lighters from New Inlet to this creek and evaporated by artificial heat, producing a fine white salt at a small expense. These Salt Works lined the coast from Cape Fear to Cape Lookout, and many were owned by speculators who made large fortunes in Confederate money from their product. Nearly all of them were demolished from time to time by the Federal blockaders which threw shells in the woods every day where tell-tale smoke indicated the location of salt pans. But as soon as the demoralized darkies who attended them could be brought back from a seven-mile stampede, the plucky owners would begin to lay out another plant.

It is also noteworthy that the bricks which were used in the original construction of Fort Caswell were made on the banks of Walden Creek.

Snow's Marsh—Dredging Steamer "Cape Fear."

Farther down is Snow's Marsh, through which the ship channel runs. This tortuous course has for years perplexed and discomfited navigators on account of the shifting sands and shoaling water which made it at times almost impassable to large vessels. For a long time this trouble baffled the engineers, but in 1895 Major W. S.

Stanton, Corps of United States Engineers, undertook to protect the channel by a training dike or wall of brushwood bound in bundles by heavy wire, which has proved highly effective. The bundles were 22 feet long and 2 feet in diameter, piled to a height of half tide between piles driven 15 feet into sand and mud, 8 feet apart, in two rows, 5 to 6 feet apart. Should this means prove permanently effective, a more substantial wall may be built later.

Another helpful contrivance of Major Stanton's is the U. S. dredging steamer "Cape Fear," which he designed especially for this service and which began a most successful work in June, 1895. She is fitted with sand-pumps of great strength and capacity, which lift and deposit in the bins on board about 500 cubic yards of sand per hour. This steamer is invaluable to the work now under the direction of Colonel D. P. Heap, U. S. Engineers, for the deepening of the river and bar.

The total expenditure of money upon our river and harbor improvement from the year 1829 to 1895 was $2,427,584.46, and Congress has just appropriated the further sum of $195,000 for the continuance of the work.

Price's Creek Light House—Confederate States Signal Station.

WE see on the Western side the old ante-bellum light-house and keeper's residence on Price's Creek, which were used during the Civil War as a signal station—the only means of communication between Fort Caswell at the western bar and Fort Fisher at the New Inlet via Smithville, where the Confederate General resided.

The Confederate States Signal Corps frequently rendered some very efficient service to the blockade-runners after they had succeeded in getting between the blockaders and the beach, where they were also in danger of the shore batteries until their character became known to the forts.

As the signal system developed, a detailed member was sent out with every ship, and so important did this service become that signal officers, as they were called, were occasionally applied for by owners or captains of steamers in the Clyde or at Liverpool before sailing for Bermuda or Nassau to engage in running the blockade.

The first attempt to communicate with the shore batteries was a failure, and consequently the service suffered some reproach for awhile, but subsequent practice with intelligent, cool-headed men, resulted in complete success, and some valuable ships, with still more valuable cargoes, were saved from capture or destruction by the intervention of the Signal Service, when, owing to the darkness and bad landfall, the captain and pilot were alike unable to recognize their geographical position.

To Mr. Frederick Gregory, of Crowells, N. C., belongs the honor of the first success as a signal operator in this service. Identified with the corps from the beginning of the blockade, and with the Cape Fear at Price's Creek Station, which was for a long time in his efficient charge, he brought to this new and novel duty an experience and efficiency equalled by few of his colleagues and surpassed by none. It was well said of him that he was always ready and never afraid—two elements of the almost unvarying success which attended the ships to which he was subsequently assigned. It was my good fortune to be intimately associated with Mr. Gregory for nearly two years, during which we had many ups and downs together as shipmates aboard and as companions ashore. He was one of the few young men engaged in blockade-running who successfully resisted the evil influences and depraved associations with which we were continually surrounded. Unselfish and honorable in all his relations with his fellows, courageous as a lion in time of danger, he was an honor to his State and to the cause which he so worthily represented.

Another gallant Confederate deserving honorable mention was Leo Vogel, an officer under Maffitt on the corvette "Florida," and subsequently with us on the "Lilian." Patriotic, brave, generous, he was a noble type of Southern chivalry, an honor to his flag and country. Of charming physique and pleasing address, his modesty and good breeding were in striking contrast with the occasionally disgraceful conduct of others who were most discreditable to the South. For some time after the war Captain Vogel was identified with the Charleston and Florida Steamboat Company, commanding for many years the steamer "Dictator," until he was placed in charge of the magnificent steamer "St. Johns," the most palatial boat ever constructed for the Florida business. While with this Company Captain Vogel numbered his friends and acquaintances by the thousands, and now that he has a steamer on the St. John's, they never fail to avail themselves of a trip with him up this beautiful river. He is said to be one of the attractions of the "Land of Flowers."

Wilmington and Charleston Mail Boats.

The ruined light-houses at Big Island, Orton Point and Price's Creek remind us of the days long ago, when passengers and mails from the great North and South were transported between Wilmington and Charleston by way of the Cape Fear river on the regular line of ocean steamers connecting the Wilmington & Weldon Railroad with Charleston and the South. The names of these steamers, which were of the best design in those days, were "Wilmington," "Gladiator," "North Carolina," "Vanderbilt" and "Dudley." The average passage between Wilmington and Charleston was about seventeen hours, but it was done under exceptionally favorable conditions in twelve hours. The boats were about 190 feet long, draft 10 to 12 feet, and in consequence of the lack of water on the bar, they had often to wait for a tide.

The Company's office and landing pier was just north of the Champion Compress, where the Atlantic Coast Line warehouses now stand. John A. Taylor, Esq., Col. James T. Miller and Captain Benjamin Lawton were agents of the line at different times; the last named acted in that capacity when the boats were sold upon the completion of the Wilmington and Manchester Rail road, now the Wilmington, Columbia and Augusta Railroad.

In 1851, the remains of the lamented statesman, John C. Calhoun, were brought from the North by the Wilmington and Weldon Railroad, and conveyed to the present Custom House wharf, from which they were transported by the "Nina," a special steamer, sent from Charleston with the Committee from that city on board. The "Nina" was draped in deep mourning.

On another occasion the famous singer, Jenny Lind, known also as the Swedish Nightingale, was a passenger during the most tempestuous voyage ever encountered by these boats—a very destructive storm prevailed along the coast. The *diva* was under the management of P. T. Barnum, and the troupe consisted of sixty persons. The great singer persisted in remaining on deck during the entire trip, while the others kept below, indifferent to everything but the fact that they were distressingly sea-sick.

The Cape Fear Quarantine Station.

The following excellent editorial by Doctor Robert D. Jewett is taken from the North Carolina Medical Journal of April 5th, 1896:

"The Cape Fear river is the only marine gateway of importance by which epidemics may gain an entrance into North Carolina; and while vessels never pass up the river more than two or three miles above Wilmington, the whole State is, of course, deeply and directly interested in the efforts to prevent the introduction of infectious diseases at this port. As the poison gaining an entrance through a slight peripheral lesion passes along the lymph and circulatory channels and makes the whole organism sick, so one case of contagious disease gaining entrance through this port, away down in the southeastern corner of the State, may spread along the avenues of travel and endanger the welfare of the whole Commonwealth. And as this applies to one State it applies to the whole country; therefore the whole country is directly interested in stopping the poison at the gateway. The watchers at the port of New York protect Chicago as truly as they do New York, and those at New Orleans defend Memphis and all the cities on the Mississippi as well as New Orleans. And since the quarantine at a port of entry is intended as a protection for the whole country, it is not just that one State or city should be burdened with the expense of conducting it.

"For a number of years the quarantine at the mouth of the Cape Fear has been under the control of a Quarantine Board, consisting of three medical men, receiving their appointment from the Governor of the State. We speak of it as a Station, but it was so only nominally, for there was no plant for the disinfection of vessel and crew, and no hospital for the care of the sick or the detention of suspects. The disinfection of vessels was accomplished by burning in their holds a quantity of sulphur, while disinfection of the crew's clothing was probably never done. The fact that we have so long escaped the introduction of contagious diseases is therefore due, apparently, rather to Divine beneficence than to our own care and watchfulness.

"The Quarantine Board have long felt the great need of a well-equipped station, and with the co-operation of the City Produce Exchange succeeded in getting passed by the Legislature of 1893 a bill appropriating $20,000 for this purpose, provided the city of Wilmington would appropriate $5,000. The city refused to do its part, and the station remained unequipped.

"In February, 1893, a bill was passed in Congress granting to the Marine Hospital Service the control over all quarantines; but provided that whenever a local quarantine station complied with the minimum requirements of the United States quarantine laws, as determined by periodical inspections by officers of the Marine Hospital Service, that station should not be interfered with. The State Board of Health seeing that the effort to equip the station and keep it under the State control had failed, turned the station over to the Marine Hospital Service. An inspection was made and an appropriation of $25,000 immediately secured for building and equipping the station with modern apparatus.

"Plans were devised in the office of the Supervising Architect and the contract to build the station awarded. Dr. J. M. Eager, who has had several years experience in Marine Hospital Service at Cincinnati, Key West and New Orleans, besides several details for special quarantine duty, was detailed to take command of the station, and will make an efficient officer.

"The new station is located on the east side of the channel of Cape Fear river about one and one-eighth miles north of Southport. The station is to be built on a pier 600 feet long, with gangways, dock and ballast crib. The head of the pier will extend into the channel in 20 feet of water. The general plan of the pier will be in the shape of a cross, the front of which will extend towards the shoals. The Disinfecting House will be provided with the most approved scientific appliances for the mechanical and chemical cleansing of infected vessels. A sulphur furnace will be provided, with which 10 per cent. per volume strength of sulphur dioxide of gas can be evolved, a result not otherwise obtainable except by the liberation of liquified sulphur dioxide. This gas will be conducted in the holds and other parts of the vessels by means of a hose. Apparatus will also be provided for disinfection by live steam, and tanks for the storage of disinfecting solutions with appliances for their application. There will be buildings for a hospital, surgeon's quarters and attendants' quarters.

"A special landing for contagious patients, to be taken to the hospital without contact with other parts of the station, will also be provided. At present the station is being conducted for inspection only. Should any infected vessel arrive at Southport quarantine before completion of the station, it will be remanded to United States quarantine station, Blackbeard Island, Sapelo, Georgia, for proper treatment.

"The inspection of vessels is always made by daylight except in cases of vessels in distress. All persons on vessels having had small-pox on board, must be vaccinated or show satisfactory evidence of recent vaccination, or of having had small-pox, or detained in quarantine for not less than fourteen days, and all effects and compartments liable to convey infection, disinfected. No fees are charged for United States quarantine. Pilots who have boarded infected vessels are subject to the same treatment as members of the crew.

"When a vessel is held for disinfection, the passengers and all of the crew are removed if cholera has occurred, save those necessary to care for the vessel. The sick are placed in hospital. Those especially suspected are carefully isolated. The others are segregated in small groups, and no communication is allowed between these groups—those being especially capable of conveying infection are not permitted to enter the barracks until they are bathed and furnished with sterile clothing. No material capable of conveying infection is taken in barracks, especially food. All hand-baggage is disinfected. All cargo liable to convey infection, the living apartments, furniture and such other portion of vessels as are liable, are disinfected. The water-tanks or casks are chemically cleansed and afterwards filled with water known to be absolutely pure, or with water recently boiled.

"After completion of all disinfection all persons are detained in quarantine for a time sufficient to cover the period of incubation of the disease for which quarantine is practiced—this for yellow fever is five days; for typhus, not less than twenty; for small-pox, not less than fourteen. No alien lepers are allowed to land. The quarantine laws will be rigidly enforced here as soon as the station is equipped."

Southport—Governor Smith—Cape Fear Pilots.

"Near the mouth of the beautiful Cape Fear river, on its right bank, is a pleasant little town. It is fanned by the delicious sea breezes; huge live-oaks gratefully shade its streets. In its sombre cemetery repose the bodies of many excellent people. Its harbor is good. It is on the main channel of the river. From its wharves can be seen, not far away, the thin white line of waves as they break on the sandy beach. But the ships to and from its neighbor, Wilmington, pay little tribute as they pass and repass. Its chief fame is that it contains the Court House of the county of Brunswick. Its name is Smithville."

Thus wrote the Hon. Kemp P. Battle, in his beautiful tribute to the memory of the first benefactor of the State University, Benjamin Smith, who had served in his youth as Aid-de-Camp of Washington, who had behaved with conspicuous gallantry under Moultrie, when he drove the British from Port Royal, who had roused to enthusiasm, by an address full of energy and fire, the entire male population of Brunswick county to follow his lead against their country's enemy, who was elected fifteen times to the Senate, and who, in 1810, became Governor of the Commonwealth. Philanthropist, Patriot, Soldier, Statesman, he came at last, in poverty and wretchedness, to a pauper's end. For him, in 1792, this charming little town was named. It was previously known as Fort Johnston, a fortification named for the Colonial Governor, Gabriel Johnston, having been established here about the year 1745 for the protection of the Colony against pirates which infested the Cape Fear.

The old garrison is still one of the sights of this healthful seaside resort. The town, or city as it is gravely called by its dignified inhabitants, is now known as Southport, and, to the credit of its virtuous citizens, it is also known as a dry town, in the sense that no intoxicants are permitted to be sold within its jurisdiction.

Smithville was a centre of busy military life during the war between the States. Here were the headquarters of the Confederate General commanding the post, and here the homes of about sixty hardy pilots whose humble sphere was suddenly exalted to the dignity of the most important and responsible officers of the swift blockade-running steamers, which braved the dangers of a hostile fleet and crept in every night under cover of the darkness.

The Cape Fear pilots have long maintained a standard of excellence in their profession most creditable to them as a class and as individuals.

The writer, for eight years a member of the Board of Commissioners of Navigation and Pilotage, having ample means of observation at home and abroad, believes that our pilots would compare most favorably with any organization of the kind elsewhere in all the essential qualifications of this noble calling.

The story of their wonderful skill and bravery in the time of the Federal blockade has never been written because the survivors are modest men, and time has obliterated from their memories many incidents of this extraordinary epoch in their history.

Amidst the impenetrable darkness, without lightship or beacon, the narrow and closely-watched inlet was felt for with a deep sea lead as a blind man feels his way along a familiar path; and even when the enemy's fire was raking the wheel-house, the faithful pilot, with steady hand and iron nerve, safely steered the little fugitive of the sea to her desired haven. It might be said of him as it was told of the Nantucket skipper, that he could get his bearings on the darkest night by a taste of lead.

Bald Head—Pirates.

BALD HEAD, upon which now stands the friendly lighthouse, an emblem of peace and good will to men, was once the scene of barbarous atrocity. In the early days of the colony, and after the abandonment of the river settlements by the whites, the Cape was in great disrepute on account of the savage barbarity of the Indians, who decoyed vessels ashore, and who, after plundering the ships, fiendishly mutilated and murdered the unfortunate sailors who fell into their hands.

It was also for years after, the rendezvous of pirates —as many as twenty piratical vessels, under the black flag, skull and cross bones, having anchored at one time in the now peaceful harbor of Southport. These preyed upon the shipping between Charleston and the West Indies; and they were commanded by the notorious pirate chiefs, Steed Bonnett and Richard Worley. The infamous Edward Teach, known as Blackbeard, also used these waters in his nefarious undertakings. He commanded a ship of forty guns and his squadron consisted of six vessels. The depredations of these sea robbers became so alarming that Governor Spotswood, of Virginia, appealed to the British naval officers on that station to send a force into Carolina waters and capture those desperate pirates. Two sloops of war were at once fitted out and a brave British officer, Lieutenant Maynard, placed in command, who sailed from James River, November 1718, and overtook Teach in Pamlico. As Maynard approached Teach, the pirate swore at him with the most horrid imprecations, saying that he would neither give nor take quarter. Maynard's ship unfortunately grounded, giving Teach the advantage, and the pirate's first broadside killed twenty of his men. Maynard saw that the situation was desperate, and promptly determined to fight hand to hand to the death. Teach immediately laid his ship alongside and boarded and the slaughter began. The deck was soon slippery with blood. Not a man on either side escaped unhurt; nearly all the pirates were killed or desperately wounded. Maynard and Teach fought hand to hand with their dirks. At last the pirate fell and the gallant Maynard, having ordered the pirate's head severed from his body, placed it at the end of his bowsprit and returned to Virginia.

On Bald Head is now established, in striking contrast with those dreadful times, a well-equipped Life Saving Station, with a sturdy crew of brave hearts and strong arms, always alert for signals of distress at sea.

The honored and lamented George Davis has eloquently referred to this point, as follows:

"Looking then to the Cape for the idea and reason of its name, we find that it is the Southermost point of Smith's Island, a naked, bleak elbow of sand, jutting far out into the ocean. Immediately in its front, are the Frying Pan Shoals pushing out still further twenty miles to sea. Together they stand for warning and for woe; and together they catch the long majestic roll of the Atlantic as it sweeps through a thousand miles of grandeur and power from the Arctic towards the Gulf. It is the play-ground of billows and tempests, the kingdom of silence and awe, disturbed by no sound save the sea-gull's shriek and the breaker's roar. Its whole aspect is suggestive, not of repose and beauty, but of desolation and terror. Imagination cannot adorn it. Romance cannot hallow it. Local pride cannot soften it. There it stands to-day, bleak and threatening and pitiless, as it stood three hundred years ago, when Greenville and White came near unto death upon its sands. And there it will stand bleak and threatening and pitiless until the earth and the sea shall give up their dead. And as its nature, so its name, is now, always has been, and always will be the 'Cape of Fear.'"

Fort Caswell.

THE work at Fort Caswell at the mouth of the Cape Fear river was commenced by the Government in the year 1826. Major George Blaney, of the United States Engineer Corps, was in charge of it for several years until his death at Smithville (now Southport), in 1836 or 1837. He was born in Boston, Massachusetts, and was an accomplished officer. His remains were brought to Wilmington, and the Wilmington Volunteers, a uniformed Company, and the only one then existing in the town, formed at the Market dock to receive them, and escorted them to the old burial-ground adjoining St. James' church, where they were interred with military honors and where they still repose.

Major Blaney's assistant in building the fort was Mr. James Ancrum Berry, a native of Wilmington, a natural engineer, the bent of whose mind was strongly mathematical, who was thoroughly competent for the position he held and who took great pride in the work. So much so, indeed, that he had a small house erected on the river-front of the fort and resided there with his family for a year or two until the encroaching waters rendered his habitation untenable, when he returned to Smithville. He died suddenly in 1832. He was hunting with the late Mr. John Brown, and while crossing a small stream on a log he lost his footing, his gun came in contact with the log and was discharged, the contents entering his brain, killing him almost instantly. He was an honorable gentleman, high-toned and chivalric, and was greatly mourned.

It is probable that Captain A. J. Swift, son of the distinguished Chief of the Engineer Corps, General Joseph Swift, succeeded Major Blaney. It is known, however, that he had charge of the works at the mouth of the river for quite a long time, and it is believed they were finished under his supervision.

Captain Swift was regarded as one of the ablest engineer officers in the Army, and, though dying quite young, left behind him a reputation second to none in that branch of the service.

Fort Caswell, named in honor of Richard Caswell, first Governor of the State, was in charge of United States Sergeant James Reilly at the beginning of the Civil War, who surrendered to a large force of Confederates under Colonel J. J. Hedrick, of Wilmington.

It is a remarkable fact that, notwithstanding its exposed position to the Federal fleet, no general engagement occurred at Caswell during the four year's war. The fort was of great service, however, in defending the main bar and the garrison at Smithville, although the fighting was confined to an occasional artillery duel with the United States blockading fleet.

The ruins are very interesting and are of a totally different character from the earthworks at Fort Fisher. It is understood that the War Department will restore and reinforce this once formidable fortification.

We learn from the "Literary Digest" of April 25th, 1896, that, with practical unanimity, the House of Representatives passed the Fortifications Appropriation Bill without a division, and in the form recommended by the Appropriations Committee, on April 14th. The bill carries a total of $5,842,337, of which $1,885,000 is for the construction of gun and mortar batteries and fortifications, and $1,729,000 for armament of fortifications. In addition to the total direct appropriation carried by the bill, the Secretary of War is authorized to enter into contracts to the total amount of $5,542,276 for materials and construction of fortifications and armament, making the aggregate amount appropriated and authorized $11,384,613.

Evacuation and Explosion of Fort Caswell.

THE defences of Oak Island were composed of Forts Caswell and Campbell, the latter a large earth fort, situated about one mile down the beach from Fort Caswell; Battery Shaw, and some other small works, all under the command of Colonel Charles H. Simonton. With Colonel Simonton were the following members of his staff: Captain E. S. Martin, Chief of Ordnance and Artillery; Captain Booker Jones, Commissary; Captain H. C. Whiting, Quartermaster, and Captain Booker, Assistant Adjutant General.

Fort Fisher fell about nine o'clock Sunday night, January 15th, 1865, and by midnight orders had been received at Fort Caswell to send the garrisons of that Fort and Fort Campbell down the beach and into the woods before daylight in order to conceal them from the Federal fleet. The troops were immediately withdrawn from the forts, and under cover of darkness marched away. Orders were also received to spike the guns in those two forts and destroy the ammunition as far as possible. Accordingly, during Monday, the 16th of January, the Chief of Ordnance and Artillery (Captain E. S. Martin) was employed with the ordnance force of the forts in carrying out this order, preparing to burn the barracks—large wooden structures built outside and around Fort Caswell—and blow up the magazines.

About one o'clock, A. M., Tuesday, January 17th, the order came to evacuate and blow up the magazines, when Colonel C. H. Simonton, Lieutenant Colonel John D. Taylor and Captain Booker Jones, who had remained up to this time, departed, leaving Captain Martin to destroy the barracks and forts. The buildings without the fort and the citadel within were at once set on fire, and were soon blazing from top to bottom. Trains had been laid during the day to each of the seven magazines at Fort Caswell and the five magazines in Fort Campbell, and under the lurid glare of the burning buildings the match was applied to the trains and magazine after magazine exploded with terrific reports. One of the magazines in Fort Caswell contained nearly one hundred thousand pounds of powder, and when it exploded the volume of sound seemed to rend the very heavens, while the earth trembled and shook, the violence of the shock being felt in Wilmington, thirty miles distant, and even at Fayetteville, more than one hundred miles away. The sight was grand beyond description. Amidst this sublime and impressive scene the flag of Fort Caswell was for the last time hauled down and carried away by the officer above mentioned, who, with his men, silently departed—the last to leave the old fort, which for four long years of war had so gallantly guarded the main entrance to the river.

War Department Records—Forts Johnston and Caswell.

SINCE the foregoing sketches of Forts Johnston and Caswell were in type I have received the following official particulars from the Honorable the Secretary of War, which will doubtless be found valuable and interesting:

"Fort Caswell, at the mouth of Cape Fear river. North Carolina, was commenced in the year 1826, the first appropriation for its construction being under Act of Congress approved March 2d, 1825. It was reported as about completed by Captain Alexander J. Swift. United States Engineers, October 20, 1838, at a total cost of $473,402. From 1838 to 1857, for preservation of site, repairs, etc., at Fort Caswell, and some repairs at Fort Johnston, the sum of $69,422.09 was expended, making a total to 1857 of $542,844.09. It was named Fort Caswell by War Department Order No. 32, of April 18th, 1833.

"Fort Caswell was an inclosed pentagonal work, with a loop-holed scarp wall, flanked by caponniers, was constructed for an armament of 61 channel-bearing guns, mounted en-barbette, and a few small guns for land defense. Capacious defensive barracks called a citadel occupied a large part of the parade.

"Upon its evacuation by the Confederate forces in January, 1865, an attempt was made to blow it up. All the scarp wall of the southeast face was overturned by a mine exploded in the scarp gallery of that face; a portion of the scarp wall of north and west fronts was badly shattered by the explosion of a magazine on the covered way near the northwest salient, and the citadel on the parade of the work was burned.

"It is now in a dilapidated condition—its armament consists of seven 10-inch and four 8-inch Columbiads and one 9-inch Dahlgren guns, all en-barbette and not mounted.

"New works are contemplated for the site of this fort, but their details are not published."

Fort Johnston, N. C.

"THE erection of the original fort was provided for by an Act of the Colonial Assembly held at New Berne April 20th, 1745 (page 94 of the Laws of North Carolina). It recited that, 'Whereas from the present War with *France* and *Spain*, there is great reason to fear that such parts of this Province which are situated most commodious for shipping to enter, may be invaded by the enemy; and whereas the entrance of *Cape Fear River*, from its known depth of water and other conveniences of navigation may tempt them to such an enterprise while it remains in so naked and defenceless a condition as it now is: Therefore, for the better securing of the Inhabitants of the said river from any insult and invasion,' etc. * * * That the 'Fort or Battery shall be called Johnston's Fort, and shall be large enough to contain at least Twenty-four Cannon, with Barracks and other conveniences for Soldiers.'

"This was before the opening of New Inlet. This opening, which was caused by a violent equinoctial storm in 1761, increased in importance, so as to form a new mouth for the Cape Fear River, deepening from 6 feet at low water in 1797 to 10 feet at low water in 1839, had a marked effect upon that river, diminishing the depth of water upon the main bar entrance from 15 feet in 1797 to 9 feet in 1839. Prior to the opening of New Inlet, and even until 1839, Baldhead channel was the natural and main entrance to the river. From 1839 to 1872 both the Rip (western channel) and New Inlet were the main entrances, and the use of Baldhead was discontinued. Since 1872 and the closure of the New Inlet, Baldhead has again become the main channel.

"As a result of work carried on under the supervision of the Corps of Engineers in 1894 the depth of the channel at mean low water was from Wilmington, 20 miles, to Snow's Marsh 18 feet, except where shoaling had occurred at the lower extremity of Lilliput Shoal, where the depth was 16½ feet; at Snow's Marsh Shoal 14 feet; on the inner shoals at the bar 16 feet by a crooked channel and 14.3 feet by a straight course, and on the outer bar 16.6 feet.

"For the original depth of water, see old maps in the office of Lieutenant-Colonel D. P. Heap, Corps of Engineers, in the Post Office building at Wilmington. For historical sketches of the work of improving that river, &c., see report of Captain C. B. Phillips, Corps of Engineers, pages 321-331, of Annual Report of the Chief of Engineers for 1876; report of Captain W. H. Bixby, Corps of Engineers, pages 1,004-1,011 of Annual Reports of the Chief of Engineers for 1886; various reports of Mr. Henry Bacon in the Annual Reports of the Chief of Engineers from 1876 to 1890, and an article on the subject published on pages 236-246 of Volume XXIX, (July, 1893, number) of the Transactions of the American Society of Civil Engineers, in a paper entitled 'The Improvement of the Harbors on the South Atlantic Coast of the United States.' The printed annual reports of the Chief of Engineers may be seen in Colonel Heap's office.

"In a report made by Acting Assistant Surgeon, S. S. Boyer, U. S. Army, on this fort, published on pages 92-94 of Circular No. 4, War Department, Surgeon General's Office, December 5th, 1870, a report on Barracks and Hospitals, with descriptions of Military Posts, he states: 'This fort receives its name from Gabriel Johnston, who was Governor of the Province of North Carolina from 1734 to 1752. It was erected by the British soon after France declared war against England, in 1744. Since that period it has been garrisoned at irregular intervals." * * *

"There is no fort built upon the reservation. During the late civil war it came into the possession of the rebels, and they constructed some minor works upon it, which have since been removed by United States troops.

"By reference to American State Papers, Military Affairs, Vol. 1, pages 95-101, 224, 237, etc., Mr. Sprunt will find information that may be of use to him in relation to the construction by the United States of a new work on the site of the old fort, finished about the year of 1809, etc. The new work consisted of a simple epaulement of concrete (some of it yet remains) and an enclosure of planks; within the enclosure there was a block house, lately destroyed, to the regret of this Department, a powder magazine, and quarters for officers of brick; and a barracks, a guard-house and a store-house of wood.

"The terreplein of the battery was ten feet below the parade and site of the buildings. The battery could receive eleven or twelve guns. The block house was square and of two stories, the upper projected three feet, forming a machicoulis defense of the approach to the lower story. The distance from the block house to the battery was about one hundred yards. This battery was provided with loop holes and embrasures above.

"There is a drawing on file entitled 'Fort Johnston and part of the town of Smithville, N. C., 1802,' which shows a large pentagonal work. Whether this represents the fort erected about 1745 or one erected later, is not shown by an examination of the records.

"This is about all the information than can be ascertained from the records and maps of this office relative to these two forts, in reference to the inquiries of Mr. Sprunt."

Wild Pigeons—Wreck of Spanish Ship. Probable Murder—Treasure Trove.

During the early part of the century, about the year 1812, great numbers of wild pigeons frequented Bald Head, where there was an immense roost. General Swift, then in command of Fort Johnston, says in his memoirs that some of these flocks were miles in extent and that the sound of their wings was like that of a roaring wind. Many were killed by sportsmen.

In November, 1803, a large Spanish ship called the "Bilboa," was cast away on Cape Fear in a storm. The crew, numbering twenty men of villainous aspect, were arrested by Lieutenant Fergus, at Fort Johnston, and confined in the block house (which still exists), under suspicion of having murdered their captain and mate at sea. They told the improbable story that their officers had died at sea, and that they, being ignorant of navigation, had let the ship drive before the wind until she fetched up on Bald Head. They all had silver dollars tied in their sashes around their waists, and they said there was a great deal more on the wreck. The pilots and others made search for this treasure but did not recover it. For fifty years afterwards, these silver coins were occasionally washed up by the sea, and the pilots living on the island were always on the alert for specie on the beach after a severe storm.

The sailors were sent to Charleston for trial, and in the absence of testimony against them, were discharged.

Monitor Nantucket.

LIFE-SAVING STATION.

Life-Savers.

About a mile from Fort Caswell, facing the dangerous middle-ground upon which many a gallant ship has met her doom, is situated the Oak Island Life-Saving Station, the crew of which patrol the beach south of main bar, while their fellow life-savers of the Cape Fear Station on Bald Head watch the white line of breakers for miles to the north.

A visit to either of these well-equipped stations will greatly interest those who are not already familiar with the drill and appliances of this humane institution. They were established upon our dangerous coast some years ago mainly through the instrumentality of our member of Congress, Colonel Alfred M. Waddell, who has said with reference to the service:

"It is a hard life, a most trying and hazardous employment, the pecuniary compensation for which, as to the surfmen, is small, and as to the keepers, who have great responsibilities, totally inadequate, being only $200 a year. If you have ever been in the breakers, as I have, even in ordinary weather and in a good boat, you can appreciate the value of calm, steady nerves, courage, strength and self-possession.

"But when a howling tempest is raging, and the waves leap heavenward (with the thermometer perhaps at zero), the men who launch a life-boat in the surf, and pull out into the hell of waters to save their fellow-beings, must be made of such stuff as heroes are made of."

A Run to Sea.

𝔓ERHAPS the air is balmy and the trip to-day includes a run to sea. We swiftly pass Fort Caswell on the starboard side, with Bald Head Light House close aport. Soon the long ground-swell of the majestic ocean tells us we have crossed the bar. Ahead we hear the dong, dong of the restless bell buoy, a weird but welcome warning to incoming strangers that dangerous shoals are near. Far off in the dim horizon, also in nearer view, white-winged merchantmen speed on their voyage up and down the coast. A trail of smoke marks the track of a distant steamer. Sea gulls, which Coleridge likened to human souls in the mist and darkness, sail past us with a grace and beauty of flight that is not of earth, but that comes alone from Him who marks the sparrow's fall and who holds the ocean in His fist.

Away to the southwest are the blackfish shoals, where many a seasick amateur has longed to be at home. Exposed to the fury of every storm on the edge of the dangerous Frying Pan, we see the faint outlines of the good Light Ship as she plunges to her mushroom anchors and buries her head in the foam.

"Alone on the wide, wide sea, so lonely 'twas that God Himself scarce seem-ed there to be."

We are now about ten miles out. Beneath us many fathoms deep reposes a gallant and ill-fated ship, the Cuban steamer "Virginius." It is a sad but o'er true tale, and it may interest the sympathizers of Cuba Libre.

Captain Fry and the Cuban War.

IN the year 1841, a winsome, honest lad, who had determined to join the navy of his country, and who had been thwarted in his purpose by the friends at home, made his way alone from Florida to Washington, and demanded his right to speak with the President, which was not denied him.

Mr. Tyler was so pleased by the youthful manliness of the little chap, who was only eight years old, that he invited him to dine at the White House on the following day. The favorable impression was confirmed on that occasion. The young Floridian was the observed of all observers; members of the Cabinet and their wives, members of Congress and officers of the navy had heard of the little lad's story, and all united in espousing his patriotic cause.

The President, won by his ardor, as well as by his gentlemanly and modest behavior, granted the boy's request and immediately signed his warrant as a midshipman in the United States Navy.

The subsequent record of Captain Joseph Fry, the Christian gentleman, the gallant sailor, the humane commander, the chivalrous soldier, is known to readers of American history. Of heroic mould and dignified address, he was

> "A combination and a form indeed,
> Where every god did seem to set his seal,
> To give the world assurance of a man."

When the Civil War came, it found him among the most beloved and honored officers in the service. The trial of his faith was brief and bitter. He could not fight against his home and loved ones, much as he honored the flag which he had so long and so faithfully cherished. He was a Southron, and with many pangs of sincere regret he went with his native State for weal or woe.

His personal bravery during the war was wonderful; he never performed deeds of valor under temporary excitement, but acted with such coolness and daring as to command the admiration of superiors and inferiors alike. He was severely wounded at the battle of White River, and while on sick leave was ordered, at his own request, to command the Confederate blockade-runner "Eugenie," upon which the writer made a voyage. On

one occasion the "Eugenie" grounded outside of Fort Fisher, while trying to run through the fleet in daylight. The ship was loaded with gun-powder—the Federal fleet was firing upon her—the risk of immediate death and destruction to crew and ship was overwhelming. Fry was ordered by Colonel Lamb to abandon the vessel and save his crew from death by explosion. He accordingly told all who wished to go—as for himself, he would stand by the ship and try to save the powder, which was greatly needed by the Confederate Government. Several boatloads of his men retreated to the fort; a few remained with Fry, the enemy's shells falling thick and fast around them. In the face of this great danger, Fry lightened his ship, and upon the swelling tide brought vessel and cargo safely in.

Later on he commanded the steamer "Agnes E. Fry," named in honor of his devoted wife. In this ship he made three successful voyages, after which she was unfortunately run ashore by her pilot, and lies not far distant from the "Virginius." Captain Fry was then placed in active service during the remainder of the war in command of the Confederate gun-boat "Morgan," and was highly complimented by his General, Dabney H. Maury, for conspicuous bravery in action.

After the war his fortunes underwent many changes. Several undertakings met with varying success or failure.

At last, he went to New York in July, 1893, where he hoped to secure employment in command of an ocean steamer. There he was introduced to General Quesada, agent of the Cuban Republic, who offered him the command of the steamer "Virginius," then lying in the harbor of Kingston, Jamaica. He accepted the offer, and received a month's pay in advance, one hundred and fifty dollars, two-thirds of which he sent to his needy family, and reserved the remainder for his personal outfit. The "Virginius," originally named "Virgin," was built in Scotland in 1864, and was especially designed for a blockade runner in the Confederate service. She made several successful trips between Havana and Mobile. Being shut up in the latter port, she was used by the Confederates as a despatch and transport steamer. For a time, after the war, she was used by the Federal Government in the United States Revenue Service, but proving unsatisfactory, owing to her great consumption of coal, was sold at public auction by the United States Treasury Department to an American firm. The owners in 1870 took out American papers in legal form, and cleared her for Venezuela. From that time she was used in conveying volunteers and supplies to Cuba; and while engaged in this business under the American flag, recognized by American consuls as an American vessel, she was overhauled at sea on the 31st of October,

1873, by the Spanish man-of-war "Tornado," and declared a prize to the Spanish Government. Fry never dreamed of greater danger—he occupied the same position he had assumed while running the Federal blockade and the same as in the recent cases of the "Commodore" and the "Bermuda." He was a merchantman, carried no guns, made no armed resistance and flew the American flag. Notwithstanding all this, a drum-head Court-Martial was held on board the "Tornado" on the second day afterwards, the unfortunate victims condemned as pirates and sentenced to immediate execution at Santiago de Cuba, where the Spanish war ship had arrived. Even then Captain Fry and his crew, who were nearly all Americans, expected release through the intervention of the United States authorities. Vain hope! The American Consul was absent; the Vice-Consul did what he could, in vain; the Home Government was silent; the British Consul protested, but without avail, and the butchery of these brave men began. We read from the newspaper accounts of the dreadful scene that the victims were ranged facing a wall. Captain Fry asked for a glass of water, which was given him by the friendly hand of one of his own race. He then walked with firm, unfaltering steps, to the place assigned him, and calmly awaited the volley which ended his noble life.

A touching scene occurred on the march to execution. When the brave man passed the American Consulate, he gravely saluted the bare pole, which should have borne the flag, once and again, so dear to his heart, but which had failed him in his extremity.

Although the firing party was only ten feet away, says the published account. Fry was the only one killed outright. Then ensued a horrible scene. "The Spanish butchers advanced to where the wounded men lay, writhing and moaning in agony, and placing the muzzles of their guns in the mouths of their victims, shattered their heads into fragments. Others were stabbed to death with knives and swords."

Fifty-three victims had suffered death—ninety-three more were made ready for execution; the bloody work was to be resumed, when an unlooked-for intervention came. The news had reached Jamaica, and it found in the harbor the British man-of-war "Niobe," under command of Captain Sir Lambton Lorraine, who, true to her name (goddess of tears) and to his instincts and honor as an Anglo-Saxon, needed no orders to speed to the rescue. Leaving in such haste that many of his men were left behind, he steamed with forced draught to Santiago. Before the anchor reached the bottom of the harbor the "Niobe's" drums had beat to quarters and the well-trained gunners were at their stations.

Commander Lorraine ignored the customary formalities; precious lives were trembling in the balance; moments were vital. Before the Spanish General was made aware of his arrival, Lorraine stood before him, and demanded that the execution be stayed. To Burriels' unsatisfactory response the brave Commander returned answer that in the absence of an American man-of-war, he would protect the interest of the Americans. Brave words, Captain Lorraine! All honor to you for them! Still the Spaniard hesitated — he had tasted human blood, but his thirst was not satisfied. Again the gallant Britisher demanded an unequivocal answer, and report says, confirmed it by a threat that he would bombard the town as he had in Honduras for the protection of the Anglo-Saxon. His prompt, decisive action arrested the bloody work, and eventually saved the lives of the remainder of the "Virginius'" crew.

On his return to England, some months later, Sir Lambton was detained some days in New York. The city authorities, animated by his gallant conduct, tendered him a public reception, which was modestly declined. Virginia City, Nevada, desiring to testify its appreciation of his noble humanity, forwarded to him a fourteen-pound brick of solid silver, upon which was inscribed his name and the incident, with the legend,

"Blood is thicker than water," signifying also, in Western eulogy, "you'r a brick."

A tardy recognition of the rights of American possession was made later by the Spanish Government, and the "Virginius" delivered to an American man-of-war. While towing the unfortunate craft off Cape Fear and bound for a Northern port, the "Virginius" sprang a-leak, or some say, was scuttled, and found her grave in the ocean-depths beneath us.

(See Life of Captain Fry, by Jeannie Mort Walker.)

Cape Fear Privateers
In the War of 1812 and 1861.

The war against Great Britain was declared on the 18th of June, 1812, and the United States were very successful on the high seas in several naval engagements, but it was the privateers which were fitted out under letters of marque that did the most damage. They severely distressed the enemy's commerce, and during the first seven months of the war captured about five hundred of their merchantmen and took nearly three thousand prisoners. The prizes taken by those "skimmers of the seas" were generally carried into the port nearest the scene of action, and sold with whatever cargoes they had, and immense sums were realized. Several were brought into Wilmington, having been captured near the coast; and it was not long before the port became a rendezvous for vessels of that character. They would appear suddenly in the river, remain a few hours, sometimes a day or two, and then mysteriously disappear, returning again with a prize they had succeeded in capturing.

Tradition reports that on one occasion two of them came in together—the Snap Dragon, under the command of Captain Otway Burns, who had at that time a considerable amount of local notoriety; and the Kemp, commanded by Captain Almida, each accompanied by a merchant vessel they had captured. In due time the vessels and cargoes were sold, but when the proceeds of the sale were to be divided a dispute arose between the two officers, each claiming that the larger portion should belong to him, as he was more instrumental in securing the prize than the other. The quarrel waxed hot, and it was feared that they would come to blows at any moment, when the fiery Burns put an end to the discussion by challenging his antagonist to meet him on the sea and fight it out yardarm to yardarm. The challenge was promptly accepted; each vessel got under way immediately, and sailed for the appointed place of meeting;

but while manœuvering for position, a fleet of the enemy's merchantmen, under convoy of a ship of war, hove in sight, and effectually put a stop to the contemplated duel. Adjourning their quarrel to another time (but which was never renewed), they dashed into the fleet and succeeded in capturing two or three ships with valuable cargoes, and brought them safely into port, a much better result in every way than trying to send each other to the bottom on a mere question of dollars and cents.

As showing how profitable the business was to all engaged in it, it is remembered that on one occasion a youth, in fact, a mere boy, who was a son of a citizen of Wilmington, volunteered on one of the ships, and was gone but one week, and his portion of the prize money amounted to more than six hundred dollars. He never tried it again, however, owing to the fact that a cannonball from one of the enemy's guns passed through his hat and slightly scalped him on its passage. He was not seriously hurt, but sufficiently so to quash any further desire on his part to become a privateersman.

In addition to the Kemp and Snap Dragon already mentioned, the waters of the Cape Fear were frequently vexed by two other craft of similar character—the Saratoga, the name of whose commander is not now attainable and the General Armstrong, Captain Sinclair, of the naval force of the United States. Quite an amusing incident is remembered in connection with Captain Sinclair, though at the time it occurred it came very near being a serious matter to him. While lying in this port, he received orders to discharge his crew and dismantle his ship, which he proceeded at once to do, and carried his light spars and rigging, ammunition and fire-arms, which latter he stacked muzzle upwards, to a building which then stood on the southeast corner of Market and Second streets, while he occupied the rooms above as an office and bed-room. This arrangement continued undisturbed for some time, but one night during the prevalence of a violent thunder-storm, a loud explosion startled the inhabitants of the town, who rushed to the spot and found that the lightning had struck the building in which Sinclair had deposited so much combustible matter, and completely destroyed it. A rigorous search was made for Sinclair, but he could not be found, and it was finally given up upon the supposition that he had been blown to pieces; but at daylight, as two of his intimates were still searching amid the ruins, one of them finally remarked: "It is no use searching any longer; old Sinclair has gone to h— at last." A smothered voice that seemed to issue from beneath their feet was heard exclaiming: "That's a lie; come here, Jacobs, and help me out." It was Sinclair in the flesh; he had been stunned by the explosion, but with the exception of a few bruises was not seriously injured. He was soon extricated from the debris under which he had been covered, and after a few remarks about the lightning, which were more emphatic than polite, he and his chums disappeared from view and were seen no more until the following day. What finally became of him we have no means of ascertaining.

When the war between the States commenced, the entire common navy was in possession of the Federal authorities, and the Confederates had no other resort than to enlist armed ships under letters of marque. Very soon quite a number of small vessels were put in commission, and reached the high seas by running the blockade; and in less than a month more than twenty prizes were taken and run into Southern ports. These vessels sailed from Charleston, Mobile, New Orleans and Wilmington, two having been fitted out in this port. It will be remembered that the Savannah, a schooner of fifty tons, ran the blockade at Charleston in 1861, captured one brig, but was herself soon after captured by the United States ship Perry, and her officers and crew were sent to Philadelphia, where they were tried for piracy, and condemned to be executed, which was only prevented by an announcement from President Davis to Mr. Lincoln that if they were executed he would surely retaliate by the execution of an equal number of United States prisoners then in the hands of the Confederate authorities. This brought the Government at Washington to their senses, and the men were subsequently exchanged as other prisoners of war. The steamers Sumter, Nashville, Florida, Alabama and Shenandoah were fitted out by the Confederate Government; and by this little fleet millions worth of merchandise was captured, and the foreign trade of the enemy nearly driven from the ocean. But this is a matter of general history, and our business just now is with that which is more local.

The first vessel fitted out as a privateer in Wilmington was the steam tug Mariner during the summer of 1861. She was owned by a company of which the late Joseph H. Flanner was president, and was armed with one twenty-four pounder forward and two nine pounders aft, and was under the command of Captain B. W. Beery. She made a cruise on the coast of North Carolina, captured one, perhaps two, vessels, and sent them into New Berne, when she returned to Wilmington. She was afterwards used during the spring and summer of 1862 by the Confederate States Government as a guard boat on the Cape Fear river, and was under command of the late Captain Joseph Price, a Wilmington boy, who was well known and greatly esteemed by our citizens.

She then made one trip through the blockade to Nassau and back to this port, but was captured on the next outward trip.

The United States Government tug "Uncle Ben" came to Wilmington in April, 1861, and was taken possession of by the Confederate States Government. When the iron-clad "North Carolina" was built, the engines of the tug were taken out and used for that ship, the hull was sold and bought by a Mr. Power, of the firm of Power, Low & Co., who were engaged in the blockade business at that time. She was rigged as a schooner and armed with one twenty-pound Parrott gun and two nine-pound smooth bore guns. She went to sea as a privateer, cruised in the West Indies for some months, capturing three or four vessels, but only succeeded in getting one into port, owing to the rigid blockade. She was finally sold in Nassau and was lost on Hatteras in the Winter of 1865. After the seizure of the "Uncle Ben" by the Confederate authorities, her name was changed to "Retribution," and she was commanded by Captain Locke, of Nova Scotia, her first officer being Captain Joseph Price, of Wilmington. These two were the only privateers fitted out in Wilmington during our late Civil War. They did not accomplish very much, and much could not have been expected of them, for they were ordinary tug-boats improvised for the occasion, and not suited to the hazardous business in which they were employed. But they did some damage, nevertheless, and those who managed and had charge of them are justly entitled to praise for the skill and intrepidity they displayed under very embarrassing and adverse conditions.

(The foregoing has been kindly furnished me by Colonel J. G. Burr.)

RUNNING THE BLOCKADE.

Blockade-Runners.

This narrative would be incomplete without a more extended reference to blockade-running on the Cape Fear during the Civil War, in which this writer, then a lad of sixteen years of age, was engaged as purser on the steamers "North Heath," "Lilian" and "Susan Beirne." The beach for many miles North and South of Bald Head is marked still by the melancholy wrecks of swift and graceful steamers then employed in this perilous enterprise. Some of the hundred vessels engaged in this traffic ran between Wilmington and the West Indies with the regularity of mail-boats, and some, even of the slowest speed, eluding the vigilance of the Federal fleet, passed unscathed twenty, thirty and forty times, making millions for their fortunate owners. One little beauty, the "Siren," a fast boat, numbered nearly fifty voyages. The success of these ships depended, of course, in a great measure, upon the skill and coolness of their commanders and pilots. It is noteworthy that those in charge of Confederate naval officers were never taken; but many were captured, sunk or otherwise lost through no fault of the brave fellows who commanded them. There were also cases of contemptible and ludicrous cowardice on the part of officers who dearly loved to brag on shore of the perils they had passed and the dangers they had braved. Such an one commanded for a time a noted and most successful blockade-runner. He was a good navigator, but when shots from the enemy's guns fell near him, he fled ingloriously from the bridge and locked himself in his cabin, leaving his chief officer and never-failing chief engineer to extricate the ship, which their cooler heads and braver hearts accomplished with safety to all on board. The unworthy commander would then, with unspeakable audacity, relate to his admiring friends from Fort Fisher a clever story of how he had eluded the pursuing blockaders.

The names of some of the wrecks referred to may interest the traveller. The "Beauregard" and the "Venus" lie stranded on Carolina Beach; the "Modern Greece" near New Inlet; the "Antonica" on Frying Pan Shoals; the "Ella" on Bald Head; the "Spunky" and the "Georgiana McCall" on Caswell Beach; the "Hebe" and the "Dee" between Wrightsville and Masonboro. Two others lie near Lockwood's Folly bar, and others whose names are forgotten lie half buried in the sands where they may remain for centuries to come.

The loss of the "Georgiana McCall" is associated with a horrible crime—the murder of her pilot. When the ship was beached under the fire of the blockaders, Mr. Thomas Dyer did not leave with the retreating crew who sought safety ashore; he seems to have been left behind in the rush. It was known that he had a large amount of money in gold on board, and it was thought that he remained to secure it. A boat returned for him, but found his bloody corpse instead. His skull was crushed as by a blow from behind; there was no money on his person. Another man was found on board, but unhurt, who professed ignorance of his fellow. This person was the watchman, and it is said that he carried ashore a large amount of money. He was arrested on suspicion, but there was no proof. He still lives on the river, but the cause of poor Dyer's death will probably never be known until the Great Assize.

CAPTAIN JOHN NEWLAND MAFFITT.

Maffitt's Experience.

We conclude our blockade-runner's reminiscences with a few extracts from his "Tales of the Cape Fear Blockade," published originally in the "Southport Leader."

[Experiences of Captain John Newland Maffitt, C. S. N., in running the blockade at Wilmington.]

"We are ready to depart; friends bid us farewell

with lugubrious indulgence of fears for our safety, as the hazards of blockade-running had recently increased in consequence of the accumulated force and vigilance of the enemy. Discarding all gloomy prognostications, at dusk we left the harbor of Nassau. Before break of day Abaco light was sighted, a place of especial interest to Federal cruisers as the turning-point for blockade-runners. At the first blush of day we were startled by the close proximity of three American men-of-war. Not the least obeisance made they, but with shot and shell paid the early compliments of the morning.

"The splintering spars and damaged bulwarks warned us of the necessity for traveling, particularly as nine hundred barrels of gun-powder constituted a portion of our cargo. A chance shell exploding in the hold would have consigned steamer and all hands to Tophet. We were in capital running condition and soon passed out of range. Tenaciously our pursuers held on to the chase, though it was evident that the fleet Confederate experienced no difficulty in giving them the go-by. In the zenith of our enjoyment of a refreshing sense of relief, the old cry of "sail ho"! came from aloft. The look-out announced two steamers ahead and standing for us. A system of zigzag running became necessary to elude the persistent enemy. Our speed soon accomplished this object. In about three hours the Federals faded under the horizon, and our proper course for the Cape Fear was resumed. Those who needed repose retired for the indulgence. My relaxation from official cares was of brief duration, as a gruff voice called out: "Captain, a burning vessel reported aloft, sir." Repairing on deck, by the aid of a spy-glass I could distinctly see, some four miles ahead, a vessel enveloped in smoke. Though not ourselves the subjects of charity, nevertheless we were human, and as seamen cherished the liveliest sympathy for the unfortunate who came to grief on God's watery highway. Regardless of personal interest, your true Jack Tar scorns the roll of Pharisee and prides himself upon the Samaritan proclivities that fail not to succor the sufferer by the wayside.

" Increasing our speed, we quickly ran quite near to the burning vessel. She proved to be a Spanish barque, with ensign at half-mast. Out of her fore hatch arose a dense smoke. Abaft were clustered a panic-stricken group of passengers and crew. Among them several ladies were observed. An ineffectual effort had been made to hoist out the long boat, which was still suspended by the yard-arm stay tackles.

"Sending an officer aloft to keep a sharp look-out that we might not be surprised by the enemy while succoring the unfortunate, the chief mate was dispatched in the cutter to render such assistance as his professional intelligence might suggest. He found the few passengers, among whom were four ladies, much calmer than the officers and crew; the latter, in place of endeavoring to extinguish the fire, which had broken out in the forecastle compartment, were confusedly hauling upon the stay-tackle in a vain effort to launch the long boat. Our mate, with his boat's crew, passed the jabbering, panic-stricken Spaniards, and proceeded at once to the forecastle, which he instantly deluged with water, and to the astonishment of all hands, speedily subdued the trifling conflagration, which proved to have resulted from the burning of a quantity of lamp-rags that had probably been set on fire by one of the crew, who carelessly emptied his pipe when about to repair on deck. The quantity of old duds that lay scattered about Jack's luxuriously furnished apartment supplied abundant material for raising a dense smoke, but the rough construction of the vessel in this locality fortunately offered nothing inflammable, and the great sensation, under the influence of a cool head, soon subsided into a farce.

"The mate, who was much of a wag, enjoyed the

general perturbation of the passengers, particularly on ascertaining that three of the ladies hailed from Marblehead, and were returning from a visit to an uncle who owned a well-stocked sugar plantation near Sagua Le Grande, in Cuba. A Spanish vessel bound to Halifax had been selected to convey them to a British port convenient for transportation to New York or Boston, without risk of being captured by Confederate buccaneers, whom, according to Cuban rumors, swarmed over the ocean and were decidedly anthropophageous in their proclivities.

"A hail from the steamer caused our mate to make his adieus, but not before announcing himself as one of the awful Southern slave-holders they had in conversation anathematized. They could not believe that so kind and polite a gentleman could possibly be a wicked 'rebel.' 'But I am, ladies, and also a slave-owner, as is your uncle—farewell.' Instead of manifesting anger at the retort, they laughed heartily and waved their handkerchiefs in kind adieu, utterly unsuspicious of having received kindness and courtesy from a blockade-runner. We made the best of speed on our way to Wilmington.

The following day, our last at sea, proved undisturbed and pleasant. At sunset the bar bore west-northwest seventy miles distant. It would be high at half-past eleven, the proper time for crossing. Sixty miles I determined to dash off at full speed, and then run slowly for disentangling ourselves from the fleet.

"None but the experienced can appreciate the difficulties that perplexed the navigator in running for Southern harbors during the war. The usual facilities rendered by the light houses and beacons had ceased to exist, having been dispensed with by the Confederate Government as dangerous abettors of contemplated mischief by the blockaders.

"Success in making the destined harbors depended upon exact navigation, a knowledge of the coast, its surroundings and currents, a fearless approach, and banishment of the subtle society of John Barleycorn. Non-experts too often came to grief, as the many hulks on the Carolina coast most sadly attest.*

"Under a pressure of steam we rushed ahead, annihilating space and melting with excited fancy hours into minutes. Our celerity shortens the distance, leaving

---

*Captain Maffitt's reference to the necessity of exact navigation on the part of masters of blockade runners during the war, recalls to us a story told by Mark Stevenson, one of the signal corps boys, about a wonderful landfall made in the "Boston" by an old friend and shipmate, Captain John W. Carrow, who said that his meridian observation made him a few miles to the westward of Raleigh, and that while he was trying to reach the capital, a yankee came along and picked him up.   J. S.

only ten miles between us and the bar. With guiding lead, slowly and carefully we feel our way.

"'Captain,' observed the sedulous chief officer, as he strove to peer through the hazy atmosphere, 'it seems to me from our soundings that we should be very near the blockaders. Don't you think so'?

"'I do, was my response. 'Hist'! there goes a bell—one, two, three, four, five, six, seven, half-past eleven—a decidedly good calculation, and it is high water on the bar. By jove! there are two directly ahead of us, and I think both are at anchor. Doubtless others are cruising around these indicators of the channel.'

"I ordered the helm put hard a-starboard, directing the wheelman to run between the two blockaders, as it was too late to sheer clear of either. Through a bank of clouds huge grim objects grew distinctly into view and necessity forced me to run the gauntlet, trusting against hope that our transit would not arouse their vigilance. They were alert vessels, for a sparkling, hissing sound was instantly followed by the fiery train of a rocket, succeeded by the dreadful calcium light, with a radiance brilliant, though brief, as to illuminate distinctly an area of miles.

"'Heave to, or I'll sink you'! shouted a gruff, imperious voice, so near that we could fancy his speaking-trumpet projected over the steamer. 'Ay, ay, sir'! was the prompt response, and to the horror of all on board, I gave the order in a loud tone: 'Stop the engine'!

"Then was heard the boatswain's whistle, the calling away of cutters and the tramping of boat's crews. Our impetus had caused the steamer to nearly emerge from between the Federals.

"Back your engines, sir, and stand by to receive my boats,' said the same stern voice. Affirmatively acknowledging the command, I whispered loud enough for the engineer to hear me: 'Full speed ahead, sir, and open wide your throttle valve.' The movements of the paddles for a moment deceived the Federal Commander into the belief that we were really backing, but speedily comprehending the manœuvre, with very fierce execrations, he gave the order to fire. Drummond lights were burned, doubtless to aid the artillerists, but so radiated the mist as to raise our hull above the line of vision, causing the destructive missiles to play havoc with the sparse rigging instead of shattering our hull and probably exploding the nine hundred barrels of gunpowder with which General Johnston afterwards fought the battle of Shiloh. It certainly was a miraculous escape for both blockader and blockade-runner. We paused not recklessly, but at the rate of 16 knots an hour absolutely flew out of the unhealthy company who discourteously followed us with exploding shells and for some time kept up such a fusillade as to impress us with the belief that the blockaders had inaugurated a 'kilkenny cat muddle,' and were polishing off each other, a supposition I subsequently learned was partially correct.

"The breakers warned us of danger, and the smooth water indicated the channel, through which we passed in safety, and at one o'clock in the morning we anchored off the venerable village of Smithville (now Southport). Then came the mental and physical reaction, producing a feeling of great prostration, relieved by the delightful realization of having passed through the fiery ordeal in safety and freedom.

> 'If after every tempest came such calms,
> May the winds blow till they have weakened death,
> And let the laboring barks climb hills of seas
> Olympus high ! and duck again as low
> As hell's from heaven.'

"After sunrise we proceeded in all haste to Wilmington, where our cargo was quickly discharged. Having obtained our return cargo, in company with two other blockade runners, I started for Nassau, and although the sentinels of the bar presented me with affectionate souvenirs in the way of shot and shell, they did but little damage. My companions came to grief, thereby adding to the prize fund that was shared by the Government with the officers of the blockade squadron."

Mrs. Maffitt adds: "On the 10th of May, 1862, Captain Maffitt arrived in Nassau on the steamer 'Gordon,' and was there presented with a communication from Captain Bullock, Confederate Navy Agent in Europe, requesting him to take immediate charge of the gunboat 'Oreto,' afterwards christened the 'Florida,' which he had dispatched to Nassau, and hasten to sea. Fully appreciating the necessity for prompt action, Captain Maffitt surrendered the 'Gordon' and took charge of the 'Oreto,' being confirmed in the command by the Secretary of the Navy. He retained command of the 'Florida' until April or June of 1864, when the state of his health compelled him to apply for detachment, which being granted, Captain Barney became his successor. At this time the 'Florida' had been run into the harbor of Brest, France, for needed repairs. Captain Maffitt writes: 'The demand on my physical ability had been excessive, nor had I entirely recovered from the effects of yellow fever, which still clung to me, and was militating against my general usefulness. Consulting a distinguished physician in Paris, he pronounced my heart affected by tropical disease, and after putting me through a course of severe treatment, started me off for Sweden, not to rest, but to travel for my health.''

Shortly afterwards Captain Maffitt went to England, took command of a blockade-runner, "Lilian," of which Mr. James Sprunt, the compiler of these notes, was the purser, and returned to the Confederacy through the port of Wilmington. He was then ordered to relieve Captain Cooke at Plymouth, N. C., from the command of the "Albemarle," which had been so wonderfully constructed and gallantly handled by Captain Cooke in the attack on the "Southfield" and "Miami." From this duty Captain Maffitt was soon relieved and ordered to the command of the "Owl," one of the blockade-runners purchased from England by the Government. The 21st of December, 1864, found him on board the "Owl" at Wilmington, receiving her cargo of 750 bales of cotton. With three other blockade-runners in company, he started for the bar. He escaped the Federal sentinels "without the loss of a rope-yarn," though one of his companions came to grief through an accident to machinery. Their destination was St. George, Bermuda, which they reached in safety, finding several steamers loaded and anxiously awaiting news from the Federal expedition under General Butler against Fort Fisher. Through a Halifax steamer, the Northern papers apprised them of the failure of the expedition, and in company with six other steamers and many gallant spirits, the

"Owl" started on her return to Dixie, all cheered by the (to them) joyful news.

In the meantime another expedition against Fort Fisher had been fitted out under General Terry and Admiral Porter, which had been successful, and the river was in possession of the Federals.

Communicating with Lockwood's Folly, where they reported all quiet and Fisher intact, Captain Maffitt steamed for the Cape Fear. At eight o'clock it was high water on the bar, and the moon would not rise before eleven. Approaching the channel, he was surprised to see but one sentinel guarding the entrance. Eluding him, he passed in. Some apprehension was excited by a conflagration at Bald Head and non-response to his signals, but as Fort Caswell looked natural and quiet, he decided to anchor off the Fort wharf. He was immediately interviewed by the Chief of Ordnance and Artillery, E. S. Martin, and another officer, who informed him of the state of affairs and that the train was already laid for blowing up Fort Caswell. Gunboats were approaching, and in great distress Captain Maffitt hastily departed. The solitary blockader pursued him furiously for some time, and far at sea he heard the explosion that announced the fate of Caswell. As his cargo was important and much needed, Captain Maffitt determined to make an effort to enter the port of

Charleston, although he had been informed that it was more closely guarded than ever before.

The rest of the story is told in Captain Maffitt's inimitable style:

"The history of the five steamers in whose company I sailed from the harbor of St. George's is briefly told. Captain Wilkinson, the late gallant commander of the 'Chickamauga,' was too experienced and keen a cruiser to be caught in a trap. Convinced from observation that there was 'something rotten in the State of Denmark,' he judiciously returned to Bermuda. The remaining three were decoyed into New Inlet by the continuance of the Mound Light, and became easy prey under the following circumstances: First, the 'Stag,' with several English officers on board as passengers, deceived by Admiral Porter's cuteness, crossed the bar, and, as was customary, anchored under the mound, there to abide the usual visit of inspection of the boarding officer of Fort Fisher. Waiting some little time without receiving the official call, the Captain naturally concluded it had been deferred until daylight. He therefore directed the steward to serve the entertainment that had been elaborately prepared to celebrate their safe arrival in the Confederacy. The gastronomic hidalgo flourished his baton of office and escorted his guests to the festive board. In shouts of revelry and with flowing bumpers, the jocund party huzzahed for Dixie, and sang her praises in songs of adulation that made the welkin ring, and aroused the sea mews from their peaceful slumbers. A pause from exhaustion having occurred in their labor of justice to the luxurious repast gave to an English captain a desired opportunity to ventilate in appropriate sentiments his appreciation of the joyful occasion. Mysteriously rapping to enjoin attention, in the silence that followed, he solemnly arose. At a wave of his dexter, the steward, all alertness, replenished the glasses.

"'Gentlemen,' said the captain, 'after a successful voyage, fraught with interesting incidents and excitements, we have anchored upon the soil of battle-worn, grand old Dixie. We come, not as mercenary adventurers, to enlist under the banner of the Confederacy, but, like true knights-errant, to join as honorable volunteers, the standard of the bravest lance in Christendom, that of the noble, peerless Lee (cheers, hear, hear). In gaining this Palestine of our chivalrous aspirations we have successfully encountered the more than ordinary perils of the sea, in storm, the lingering chase, and hazards of the blockade. Through all vicissitudes there was a mind to conceive, a hand to guide, a courage to execute. Gentlemen, I propose the health and happiness and speedy promotion of the officer who merits these commendations—our worthy commander.'

"Mingled with vociferous applause, came the customary hip! hip! huzzah! hip! hip! huz—

"The half uttered huzzah froze like an icicle on the petrified lips of the orator, who

'With wild surprise,
As if to marble stuck, devoid of sense,
A stupid moment, motionless stood,'

as the apparition of a Federal midshipman appeared upon the cabin stairway.

"'Who commands this steamer?' was the Federal's interrogatory.

"'I am that unhappy individual,' groaned the commander, as reminiscences of a long confinement came painfully to his mind.

"'You are a prize to Admiral Porter's squadron, and I relieve you of all further responsibility. Gentlemen, as parolled prisoners, you are at liberty to finish your repast.'

"The withering enunciation of capture blighted like a black frost the hopeful blossoms that had, under the inspiring influence of the sparkling Epernay, bubbled into poetic existence. One by one the lights soon faded in this banquet hall deserted, their last glimmer, falling mournfully on the debris of the unfinished congratulatory repast.

"Ere an hour elapsed two more unfortunates, lured by the channel lights, entered and likewise anchored off the mound, and became a prey to Admiral Porter's fleet.

"My cargo being important, and the capture of Fort Fisher and Cape Fear cutting me off from Wilmington, I deemed it my duty to make an effort to enter the harbor of Charleston, in order to deliver the much-needed supplies.

"I had been informed that the blockade of that port was more stringently and numerically guarded than ever before since the inauguration of hostilities. The 'Owl's' speed was now accommodated to the necessary time of arriving off the bar, which was 10 P. M. Throughout the day vigilant steamers were seen along the shore inspecting inlets and coves regardless of their want of capacity for blockade purposes. This spirit of inspection and watchfulness was most assiduous, as if an order had been issued to overhaul even the coast gallinipers to see that aid and comfort in the shape of muskets and pistols were not smuggled into the needy Confederacy. Occasionally one of these constables of the sea would fire up and make a dash after the 'Owl'; a little more coal and stirring up of the fire-draft was sufficient to start the blockade-runner off with such admirable speed as to convince the Federal that he was after the fleetest steamer that ever eluded the guardians of the channel-ways.

"Seasonably making the passage, 9 o'clock, P. M., found us not far from the mouth of Maffitt's channel. Anticipating a trying night and the bare possibility of capture, two bags were slung and suspended over the quarter by a stout line. In these bags were placed the Government mail not yet delivered, all private correspondence, and my war journal, including the cruise of the 'Florida,' besides many other papers. An intelligent quarter-master was ordered to stand by the bags with a hatchet, and the moment capture became inevitable, to cut adrift and let them sink.

"When on the western tail-end of Rattlesnake Shoal, we encountered streaks of mist and fog that enveloped stars and everything for a few moments, when it would become quite clear again. Running cautiously in one of these obscurations, a sudden lift in the haze disclosed that we were about to run into an anchored blockader. We had bare room with a hard-aport helm to avoid him some fifteen or twenty feet, when their officer on deck called out: 'Heave to, or I'll sink you'! The order was unnoticed, and we received his entire broadside, that cut away turtle-back, perforated forecastle and tore up bulwarks in front of our engine-room, wounding twelve men, some severely, some slightly. The quarter-master stationed by the mail-bags was so convinced that we were captured that he instantly used his hatchet, and sent them, well moored, to the bottom. Hence my meagre account of the cruise of the 'Florida.' Rockets were fired as we passed swiftly out of his range of sight, and drummond lights lit up the animated surroundings of a swarm of blockaders, who commenced an indiscriminate discharge of artillery. We could not understand the reason of this bombardment, and as we picked our way out of the melee, concluded that several blockade-runners must have been discovered feeling their way into Charleston.

"After the war, in conversing with the officer commanding on that occasion, he said that a number of the steamers of the blockade were commanded by inexperienced volunteer officers, who were sometimes overzealous and excitable, and hearing the gun-boat firing into me, and seeing her rockets and signal lights, they thought that innumerable blockade-runners were forcing a passage into the harbor, hence the indiscriminate discharge of artillery, which was attended with unfortunate results to them. This was my last belligerent association with blockade-running. Entering the harbor of Charleston, and finding it in the possession of Federals,

I promptly checked progress and retreated. The last order issued by the Navy Department, when all hope for the cause had departed, was for me to deliver the 'Owl' to Frazier, Trenholme & Co., in Liverpool, which I accordingly did."

The Blockade Runner "Don."

ONE of the most distinguished Commanders of the blockade running steamers was Captain Roberts (so-called) of the twin screw steamer "Don," a quick, handy little boat, admirably adapted to the trade. I had the pleasure of knowing him personally through frequent intercourse with his signal officer, a fine young fellow, named Selden, from Virginia, and we were much impressed with the superior bearing and intelligence of this remarkable man, who afterwards became famous in the war between Russia and Turkey as Hobart Pasha, Admiral-in-Chief of the Turkish Navy.

"Captain Roberts" was really the Honorable Augustus Charles Hobart Hampden (son of the Earl of Buckinghamshire), Post Captain in the Royal Navy, and for a time Commander of Queen Victoria's yacht "Victoria and Albert." He had seen service in the war between Emperor Nicholas, France and Great Britain in 1854, under the great Admiral Sir Charles Napier, when he commanded H. M. S. "Driver," and after the general order "Lads sharpen your cutlasses" boarded the Russian warships before Cronstadt, stormed the seven forts which guarded the entrance to that harbor, and sailed up the Neva even to St. Petersburg itself. Having made several runs into Wilmington during his absence from England on leave, he returned home, and, fretting under the dull routine of service ashore, accepted the command of the entire Turkish Navy at the outbreak of the war with his old antagonists, the Russians. He died in 1886 Admiral-in-Chief of the Turkish Navy, and was buried in the English cemetery at Scutari. Following is his own account of adventures in blockade-running to Wilmington :

"We left the quay at Wilmington cheered by the hurrahs of our brother blockade-runners, who were taking in and discharging their cargoes, and steamed a short distance down the river, when we were boarded to be searched and smoked. This latter extraordinary proceeding, called for perhaps by the existing state of affairs, took me altogether aback. That a smoking apparatus should be applied to a cargo of cotton seemed almost astounding. But so it was ordered, the object being to search for runaways, and strange to say, its efficacy was apparent, when, after an hour or more application of the process (which was by no means a gentle one) an unfortunate wretch, crushed almost to death by the closeness of his hiding-place, poked with a long stick till his ribs must have been like touchwood, and smoked the color of a backwood Indian, was dragged by the heels into the daylight, ignominiously put into irons and hurled into the guard-boat. This discovery nearly caused the detention of the vessel on suspicion of our being the accomplices of the runaway; but after some deliberation we were allowed to go on.

"Having steamed down the river a distance of about twenty miles, we anchored at two o'clock in the afternoon near its mouth. We were hidden by Fort Fisher from the blockading squadron lying off the bar, there to remain till some time after nightfall. After anchoring we went on shore to take a peep at the enemy from the batteries. Its commandant, a fine, dashing young Confederate officer (Colonel Lamb), who was a firm friend to blockade-runners, accompanied us round the fort. We counted twenty-five vessels under weigh ; some of them occasionally ventured within range ; but no sooner had one of them done so than a shot was thrown so unpleasantly near that she at once moved out again.

"We were much struck with the weakness of Fort Fisher, which, with a garrison of twelve hundred men, and only half finished, could have been easily taken at any time since the war began by a resolute body of five thousand men making a night attack. It is true that at the time of its capture it was somewhat stronger than at the time I visited it, but even then its garrison was comparatively small and its defences unfinished. I fancy the bold front so long shown by its occupiers had much to do with the fact that such an attack was not attempted till just before the close of the war. The time chosen for our starting was eleven o'clock, at which hour the tide was at its highest on the bar at the entrance of the river. Fortunately the moon set about ten, and as it was very cloudy, we had every reason to expect a pitch-dark night. There were two or three causes that made one rather more nervous on this occasion than when leaving Bermuda.

"In the first place, five minutes after we had crossed the bar we should be in the thick of the blockaders, who always closed nearer in on the very dark nights. Secondly, our cargo of cotton was of more importance than the goods we had carried in; and thirdly, it was the thing to do to make the double trip in and out safely. There were also all manner of reports of the new plans that had been arranged by a zealous Commodore lately sent from New York to catch us all. However, it was of no use canvassing these questions, so at a quarter to eleven we weighed anchor and steamed down to the entrance of the river.

"Very faint lights, which could not be seen far at sea, were set on the beach in the same position as I have before described, having been thus placed for a vessel coming in; and bringing these astern in an exact line, that is, the two into one, we knew that we were in the passage for going over the bar. The order was then given: 'Full speed ahead,' and we shot at a great speed out to sea.

"Our troubles began almost immediately; for the cruisers had placed a rowing barge, which could not be seen by the forts, close to the entrance, to signalize the direction which any vessel that came out might take. This was done by rockets being thrown up by a designed plan from the barge. We had hardly cleared the bar when we saw this boat very near our bows, nicely placed to be run clean over, and as we were going about fourteen knots, her chance of escape would have been small had we been inclined to finish her. Changing the helm, which I did myself, a couple of spokes just took us clear. We passed so close that I could have dropped a biscuit into the boat with ease.

I heard the crash of broken oars against our sides; not a word was spoken.

"I strongly suspect every man in that boat held his breath till the great white avalanche of cotton, rushing by so unpleasantly near, had passed quite clear of her.

"However, they seemed very soon to have recovered themselves, for a minute had scarcely passed before up went a rocket, which I thought a very ungrateful proceeding on their part. But they only did their duty, and perhaps they did not know how nearly they had escaped being made food for fishes. On the rocket being thrown up, a gun was fired uncommonly close to us, but as we did not hear any shot, it may have been only a signal to the cruisers to keep a sharp lookout.

"We steered a mile or two near the coast, always edging a little to the eastward, and then shaped our course straight out to sea. Several guns were fired in the pitch-darkness very near us. (I am not quite sure whether some of the blockaders did not occasionally pepper each other.) After an hour's fast steaming we felt moderately safe, and by the morning had a good offing.

"Daylight broke with thick, hazy weather, nothing being in sight. We went all right till half-past eight o'clock, when the weather cleared up, and there was a large paddle-wheel cruiser (that we must have passed very near to in the thick weather) about six miles astern of us. The moment she saw us she gave chase. After running for a quarter of an hour it was evident that, with our heavy cargo on board, the cruiser had the legs of us, and as there was a long day before us for the chase, things looked badly. We moved some cotton aft to immerse our screws well; but still the cruiser was steadily decreasing her distance from us, when an incident of a very curious nature favored us for a time.

"It is mentioned in the book of sailing directions that the course of the gulf stream (in the vicinity of which we knew we were) is in calm weather and smooth water plainly marked out by a ripple on its inner and outer edges. We clearly saw, about a mile ahead of us, a remarkable ripple, which we rightly, as it turned out, conjectured was that referred to in the book. As soon as we had crossed it we steered the usual course of the current of the Gulf Stream, that here ran from two to three miles an hour. Seeing us alter our course, the cruiser did the same; but she had not crossed the ripple on the edge of the stream, and the course she was now steering tended to keep her for some time from doing so. The result soon made it evident that the observations in the book were correct; for until she, too, crossed the ripple into the stream, we dropped her rapidly astern, whereby we increased our distance to at least seven miles.

"It was now noon, from which time the enemy again began to close with us, and at five o'clock was not more than three miles distant. At six o'clock she opened a harmless fire with the Parrott gun in her bow, the shot falling far short of us. The sun set at a quarter to seven, by which time she had got so near that she managed to send two or three shots over us, and was steadily coming up.

"Luckily, as night came on, the weather became very cloudy, and we were on the dark side of the moon, now setting in the West, which occasionally breaking through the clouds astern of the cruiser, showed us all her movements, while we must have been very difficult to make out, though certainly not more than a mile off. All this time she kept firing away, thinking, I suppose, that she would frighten us into stopping. If we had gone straight on, we should doubtless have been caught, so we altered our course two points to the eastward. After steaming a short distance, we stopped quite still, blowing off steam under water, not a spark or the slightest smoke showing from the funnel; and we had the indescribable satisfaction of seeing our enemy steam past us, still firing ahead at some imaginary vessel.

"This had been a most exciting chase and a very narrow escape; night only saved us from a New York prison. All this hard running had made an awful hole in our coal-bunkers, and as it was necessary to keep a stock for a run off the Bahama Islands, we were obliged to reduce our expenditure to as small a quantity as possible. However, we were well out to sea, and after having passed the line of cruisers between Wilmington and Bermuda, we had not much to fear until we approached the British possessions of Nassau and the adjacent Islands, where two or three very fast American vessels were cruising, although five hundred miles from American waters. I am ignorant, I confess, of the laws of blockade, or indeed if a law there be that allows its enforcement and penalties to be enacted, five hundred miles away from the ports blockaded. But it did seem strange that the men-of-war of a nation at peace with England should be allowed to cruise off her ports to stop and examine trading vessels of all descriptions, to capture and send to New York, for adjudication vessels on the mere suspicion of their being intended blockade-runners; and to chase and fire into real blockade-runners so near to the shore that on one occasion the shot and shell fell into a fishing village, and that within sight of an English man-of-war lying at anchor in the harbor at

Nassau. Surely it is time that some well-understood laws should be made, and rules laid down, or such doings will sooner or later recoil on their authors.

"Having so little coal on board, we determined on making for the nearest point on the Bahama Islands, and luckily reached a queer little island called Green Turtle Quay, on the extreme North of the group, where was a small English colony, without being seen by the cruisers. We had not been there long, however, before one of them came sweeping round the shore and stopped unpleasantly near to us; even though we were inside the rock, she hovered about outside, not a mile from us.

"We were a tempting bait, but a considerable risk to snap, and I suppose the American captain could not quite make up his mind to capture a vessel (albeit a blockade-runner piped full of cotton) lying in an English port, insignificant though that port might be. We had got a large white English ensign hoisted on a pole, thereby showing the nationality of the rock, should the cruiser be inclined to question it. After many longing looks she steamed slowly away, much to our satisfaction. Coals were sent to us from Nassau the next day, which having been taken on board, we weighed anchor, keeping close to the reefs and islands all the way. We steamed towards that port, and arrived safely, having made the in-and-out voyage, including the time in unloading and loading at Wilmington, in sixteen days.

"To attempt to describe at length the state of things at this unusually tranquil and unfrequented little spot is beyond my powers. I will only mention some of its most striking features. Nassau differed much from Wilmington, inasmuch as at the latter place there was a considerable amount of poverty and distress, and men's minds were weighed with many troubles and anxieties; whereas at Nassau everything at the time I speak of was *couleur de rose*. Every one seemed prosperous and happy. You met with calculating, far-seeing men who were steadily employed in feathering their nests, let the war in America end as it might; others, who, in the height of enthusiasm for the Southern cause, put their last farthing into Confederate securities, anticipating enormous profits; some men, careless and thoughtless, living for the hour, were spending their dollars as fast as they made them, forgetting that they 'would never see the like again.' There were rollicking captains and officers of blockade-runners, and drunken, swaggering crews; sharpers looking out for victims; Yankee spies and insolent, worthless free niggers—all these combined made a most heterogeneous, though interesting, crowd.

"The inhabitants of Nassau, who, until the period of blockade-running, had, with some exceptions, subsisted on a precarious and somewhat questionable livelihood gained by wrecking, had their heads as much turned as the rest of the world. Living was exorbitantly dear, as can well be imagined, when the captain of a blockade-runner could realize in a month a sum as large as the Governor's salary. The expense of living was so great that the officers of the West India regiment quartered here had to apply for special allowance, and I believe their application was successful. The hotel, a large building, hitherto a most ruinous speculation, began to realize enormous profits. In fact, the almighty dollar was spent as freely as the humble cent had been before this golden era in the annals of Nassau.

"As we had to stay here till the time for the dark nights came round again, we took it easy, and thoroughly enjoyed all the novelty of the scene. Most liberal entertainment was provided free by our owner's agent, and altogether we found Nassau very jolly; so much so that we felt almost sorry when 'time' was called, and we had to prepare for another run. In fact, it was pleasanter in blockade-running to look backwards than forwards, especially if one had been so far in good luck.

"All being ready, we steamed out of Nassau harbor, and were soon again in perilous waters. We had a distant chase now and then —a mere child's play to us after our experience— and on the third evening of our voyage we were pretty well placed for making a run through the blockading squadron as soon as it was dark. As the moon rose at twelve o'clock, it was very important that we should get into port before she threw a light upon the subject.

"Unfortunately, we were obliged to alter our course or stop so often to avoid cruisers that we ran our time too close; for, as we were getting near to the line of blockade, a splendid, three-quarter size moon rose, making everything as clear as day. Trying to pass through the line of vessels ahead with such a bright light shining would have been madness; in fact, it was dangerous to be moving about at all in such clear weather, so we steamed towards the land on the extreme left of the line of cruisers, and having made it out, went quite close inshore and anchored.

"By lying as close as we dared to the beach, we must have had the appearance of forming part of the low sand hills, which were about the height and color of the vessel, the wood on their tops forming a background, which hid the small amount of funnel and mast that showed above the decks. We must have been nearly invisible, for we had scarcely been an hour at anchor, when a gun-boat came steaming along the shore very near to the beach; and while we were breathlessly watching her, hoping she would go past, she dropped anchor alongside of us, a little outside where we were lying—so close that we not only heard every order that was given on board, but could almost make out the purport of the ordinary conversation of the people on her decks. A pistol shot would have easily reached us. Our position was most unpleasant, to say the least of it. We could not stay where we were, as it only wanted two hours to daybreak. If we had attempted to weigh anchor, we must have been heard doing so. However, we had sufficient steam at command to make a run for it. So, after waiting a little to allow the cruiser's fires to get low, we knocked the pin out of the shackle of the chain on deck, and easing the cable down into the water, went ahead with one engine and astern with the other, to turn our vessel round head to seaward.

"Imagine our consternation when, as she turned, she struck the shore before coming half round (she had been lying with her head inshore, so now it was pointed along the beach, luckily in the right direction, i. e., lying from the cruiser). There was nothing left to us but to put on full speed, and if possible force her from the obstruction, which after two or three hard bumps we succeeded in doing.

"After steaming quite close to the beach for a little way, we stopped to watch the gun-boat, which, after resting for an hour or so, weighed anchor and steamed along the beach in the opposite direction to the way we had been steering, and was soon out of sight. So we steamed a short distance inshore and anchored again. It would have been certain capture to have gone out to sea just before daybreak, so we made the little craft as invisible as possible, and remained all the next day, trusting to our luck not to be seen. And our luck favored us, for although we saw several cruisers at a distance, none noticed us, which seems almost miraculous.

"Thus passed Christmas day, 1863, and an anxious day it was to all of us. We might have landed our cargo where we were lying but it would have been landed in a dismal swamp, and we would have been obliged to go into Wilmington for our cargo of cotton.

"When night closed in we weighed anchor and steamed to the entrance of the river, which, from our position being so well defined, we had no difficulty in making out. We received a broadside from a savage little gun-boat quite close in shore, her shot passing over us, and that was all. We got comfortably to the anchorage about half-past eleven o'clock, and so ended our second journey in.

"It is not my intention to inflict on my readers any more anecdotes of my doings in the D——n, suffice it to say that I had the good luck to make six round trips in her, in and out of Wilmington, and that I gave her over to the chief officer and went home to England with my spoils.

"On arriving at Southampton, the first thing I saw in the 'Times' was a paragraph headed 'The capture of the 'D——n.' Poor little craft! I learned afterwards how she was taken, which I will relate, and which will show that she died game.

"The officer to whom I gave over charge was as fine a specimen of a seaman as can well be imagined, plucky, cool and determined, and by the way, he was a bit of a medico, as well as a sailor; for by his beneficial treatment of his patients we had very few complaints of sickness on board. As our small dispensary was close to my cabin I used to hear the conversation that took place between C—— and his patients. I will repeat one:

C.—'Well, my man, what's the matter with you?'
Patient.—'Please, sir, I've got pains all over me.'
C.—'Oh, all over you are they; that's bad.'

"Then, during the pause, it was evident something was being mixed up, and I could hear C—— say: 'Here, take this, and come again in the evening.' (Exit patient.)

"Then C—— said to himself: 'I don't think he'll come again; he has got two drops of the croton. Skulking rascal, pains all over him, eh?'

"I never heard the voice of that patient again; in fact, after a short time we had no cases of sickness on board.

"C—— explained to me that the only medicine he served out, as he called it, was croton oil; and that none of the crew came twice for treatment.

"Never having run through the blockade as commander of a vessel (though he was with me all the time and had as much to do with our luck as I had), he was naturally very anxious to get safely through. There can be no doubt that the vessel had lost much of her speed, for she had been very hardly pushed on several occasions. This told sadly against her, as the result will show.

"On the third afternoon after leaving Nassau she was in a good position for attempting the run when night came on. She was moving stealthily about waiting for the evening, when suddenly, on the weather, which had been hitherto thick and hazy, clearing up, she saw a cruiser unpleasantly near to her, which bore down under steam and sail, and it soon became probable that the poor little 'D——n's' twin screws would not save her this time, well and often as they had done so before.

"The cruiser, a large, full-rigged corvette, was coming up hand over hand, carrying a strong breeze, and the days of the 'D——n' seemed numbered, when C—— tried a ruse worthy of any of the heroes of naval history.

"The wind, as I said, was very fresh, with a good deal of sea running.

"On came the cruiser till the 'D——n' was almost under her bows, and shortened sail in fine style. The moment the men were in the rigging, going aloft to furl the sails, C—— put his plan into execution. He turned his craft head to the wind, and steamed deliberately past the corvette at not fifty yards distance. She with great way on, went nearly a quarter of a mile before she could turn.

"I have it from good authority that the order was not given to the marines on the man-of-war's poop to fire at the plucky little craft who had so fairly out-manœuvred the cruiser, for out-manœuvred she was to all intents and purposes.

"The two or three guns that had been cast loose during the chase had been partially secured, and left so while the men had gone aloft to furl the sails, so that not a shot was fired as she went past. Shortly after she had done so, the cruiser opened fire with her bow guns, but with the sea that was running she could do no harm, being without any top weights.

"The 'D——n' easily dropped the corvette with her heavy spars astern, and was soon far ahead, so much so that when night came on the cruiser was shut out of sight in the darkness.

"After this the 'D——n' deserved escape, but it was otherwise fated.

"The next morning when day broke she was within three miles of one of the new fast vessels, which had come out on her trial trip, flying light, alas! She had an opportunity of trying her speed advantageously to herself. She snapped up the poor 'D——n' in no time and took her to the nearest port.

"I may mention that the 'D——n' and her captain were well known and much sought after by the American cruisers. The first remark that the officer on coming aboard her was: 'Well, Captain Roberts, so we have caught you at last!' and he seemed much disappointed when he was told that the captain they so particularly wanted went home in the last mail.

"The corvette, which had been chased and beaten by the 'D——n' the day before, was lying in the port into which she was taken. Her captain, when he saw the prize said, 'I must go on board and shake hands with the gallant fellow who commands that vessel!' and he did so, warmly complimenting C—— on the courage he had shown, thus proving that he could appreciate pluck and that American naval men did not look down on blockade-running as a grievous sin, hard work as it gave them to put a stop to it. They were sometimes a little severe on men who, after having been fairly caught in a chase at sea, wantonly destroyed their compasses, chronometers, etc., rather than let them fall into the hands of the cruiser's officers.

"I must say that I was always prepared, had I been caught, to have made the best of things, to have given the officer who came to take possession all that they had fairly gained by luck having declared on their side, and to have a farewell glass of champagne with the new tenant at the late owner's expense. The treatment received by persons captured engaged in running the blockade differed very materially.

"If a *bona fide* American man-of-war of the Old

School made the capture, they were always treated with kindness by their captors. But there were among the officers of vessels picked up hurriedly and employed by the Government a very rough lot, who rejoiced in making their prisoners as uncomfortable as possible. They seemed to have only one good quality, and this was that there were among them many freemasons, and frequently a prisoner found the advantage of having been initiated into the brotherhood.

"The 'D——n' crew fell into very good hands, and till they arrived at New York were comfortable enough; but the short time they spent in prison there, while the vessel was undergoing the mockery of a trial in the Admiralty Court, was far from pleasant. However, it did not last very long—not more than ten days; and as soon as they were free most of them went back to Nassau or Bermuda ready for work.

"C—— came to England and told me all his troubles. Poor fellow! I am afraid his services were not half appreciated as they ought to have been, for success, in blockade-running, as in everything else, is a virtue, whereas bad luck, even though accompanied with pluck of a hero, is always more or less a crime not to be forgiven."

Pilots in a Storm.

We have referred to the hard life of these toilers of the sea, who often win their bread at the risk of their lives.

Before the recent change in the method of boarding inward-bound vessels, pilotage business was open to general competition, and as about sixty licensed men depended upon their profession for a living, many of them took their lives in their hands and cruised in frail boats and heavy weather for fifty and a hundred miles at sea, searching for vessels in need of their assistance.

We illustrate some of the hardships to which they were exposed by the following thrilling story of the great storm in 1877 by Colonel Waddell, which will doubtless be read with interest:

"On April 12th, 1877, one of the most terrific storms that ever visited the North Carolina coast began and lasted for three days, culminating on the 15th off Cape Fear. It was fearfully destructive to life and property, wrecking many ships with their crews and cargoes, and burying them beneath the waves. One large three-masted vessel broke up and parts of her drifted into Smithville Bay, a prize for the wreckers, which not only illustrated the force of the storm, but was a curiosity in the strength of its structure.

"All her bolts," said one who examined pieces of the wreck, 'are brass, four, six and even eight feet long; the knees are solid iron and the outside planking six inches through and of stout pine'."

There were two Smithville pilot-boats, the Mary K. Sprunt and the Uriah Timmons, cruising off the coast at the time the storm commenced, and finding it impossible to make a harbor, they were compelled to stand off and try to weather it out.

The Mary K. Sprunt had a crew of five men, viz: Christopher Pinner, Robert Walker, Charles Dosher, Jr., Thomas Grissom and Lawrence Gillespie, the cook. They were brave and skilful men, but after a desperate struggle, in which all that the most skilful seamanship could accomplish had been exhausted, she went down with all on board. On the 28th, the body of Tom Grissom was found by the pilot-boat H. Westerman, floating at sea, about nine miles out, and the pilots also found the Mary K. Sprunt lying on the bottom, in eleven and a half fathoms, her white sails torn into ribbons, shining up through the blue depths and undulating with the motion of the restless sea.

The Uriah Timmons had a crew of four men, C. C. Morse, Julius Weeks, Joseph Thompson, Jr., and Joseph

Arnold, and of these Arnold was the youngest, hardly twenty years of age. Every precaution was taken upon the approach of the storm, and with only enough canvas to steer by, she faced it. All day and night of the 12th, she leaped and rolled and dived like a cork on the waves, while the storm increased in fury every hour. Day dimly dawned on the 13th over a howling waste of waters, whose billows heaved her skyward, leaving great chasms, down whose sides she rushed headlong as if to certain destruction. A gray mist shrouded sky and sea, and the storm-fiend shrieked with that unearthly voice which, once heard, is never forgotten. Cowering before the blast, licked from stem to stern by the tongue of the hungry sea, groaning and sobbing as she strained up the watery heights or slid down the hissing gulfs, the little ship drove on. Although carrying but thirteen yards of canvas, the jaw of the boom was eating into the foremast like a famished animal. With the advancing day, the fury of the gale increased. It seemed as if the spirit of an angry god walked the waters and was lashing the elements in his wrath. A mountainous wave, leading the host of billows, would rush toward the little vessel, and toppling as if to fall upon and crush her, would lower its crest, and gliding beneath her trembling timbers, lift her almost clear in air and toss her, toy-like, to another billow, while the multitudinous ocean roared with rage.

The crew of the Timmons, brave and hardy mariners as they were, and accustomed to storms on the broad water from childhood, stood appalled at the surpassing terrors of this awful scene.

Lashed in the cockpit, with vise-like grip upon the wheel and drenched to the skin, sat Julius Weeks, who had been there thirteen hours. At last, towards afternoon, to the utter dismay of all on board, the jib-halyard parted, and flying down the stay, the jib hung, bag-like, below the bowsprit, and instantly the sea, like a ravenous beast, fell upon it and held it down as if devouring it. The brave boat struggled hard to lift her bow, thus weighed, from the waves, and with a mighty effort succeeded. Again the sea seized and held the bellying jib, and again the gallant boat, struggling, raised it clear, but with weakening power. The pilots now realized that, unless immediately released from this new and frightful danger, the Timmons could not hold her head up, but must founder after a few more struggles; but, feeling assured that an attempt to reach the jib-stay would result in certain death, as no man could ever remain on the bowsprit, even if he could reach it, they were stricken with despair. "We are lost," exclaimed one; "unless we can cut that jib-halliard, we are certainly gone! A man can't live there, but it is our only hope."

Who should do this desperate deed? They hurriedly agreed to decide the matter by lot, and were about to proceed to do so, when Joe Arnold, who was now at the wheel, shouted: "Hold on, men! You are all married and have families; I am a single man: let me try it, and if I go overboard it will be all right," and surrendering the wheel, the brave boy drew his sheath-knife, and putting it between his teeth, started forward. It was impossible to keep his footing, and so he crawled cautiously along the deck (there is no railing to a pilot-boat), holding on as best he could. His companions watched him with the eagerness of men whose only hope of life hung on his steadiness of nerve and physical strength. If he reached the bowsprit in safety, the sea would certainly beat him off, for every time the little craft plunged, the waves seemed to leap up to meet her. For the first time since childhood fervent prayers rose to the lips of some of these men, who had "followed the sea" all their days without thinking of Him whose presence they now realized as they had never realized it before, and tears flowed freely down their bronzed faces.

Joe reached the foremast, and just then the Timmons rolled nearly on her beam-ends. He threw his arms around the mast and held on. The storm was now indescribably fierce and terrific. As the vessel slowly recovered herself, he loosened his hold and crawled towards the bowsprit. He reached it, got astride of it, locked his arms around it, drew a long breath, and then with a rush, the Timmons buried her head and Joe disappeared in the seething waters.

The crew held their breath in an agony of suspense, while their eyes strained towards the boiling foam which engulfed him. In a moment the staunch craft, as if conscious of the heroic effort for her relief, and stimulated by it to renewed exertion, bounded forward and upward through the dashing waters. And on the bowsprit, which was pointing skyward, the crew saw Joe straightening himself into a sitting position, the knife still held in his clenched teeth, and preparing to crawl still further out. Again and again this scene was enacted, each plunge and rise finding the hero nearer the object at which he aimed, while the crew fairly ached with the intensity of their emotions.

He reached it at last, and watching the most favorable opportunity, released his right arm, snatched the knife from his teeth, and with a swift and powerful stroke cut the jib-halliard through, as the trembling vessel started down another sea, restored the knife to its place, again clasped the bowsprit in his arms, and again disappeared, but only for a moment, for the Timmons, now relieved of the weight which held her down, sprang out of the threatening gulf as with new life inspired. It was a great relief, but the tempest was still at its height, and now both Joe and the crew realized that the most hazardous part of this heroic enterprise was still before him, namely, getting back to the deck again. It was not like coming down from aloft. He had to repeat the desperate performance backward.

Slowly, and still astride the bowsprit, and still alternately plunged in the sea and lifted high in the air, he began the fearful task. Every instant was a crisis, every moment threatened to be his last; but slowly and steadily he approached the deck.

Finally he reached it, slid along the foremast, clasped it as before, and at last, crawling, laid himself down exhausted amid his awe-struck companions.

The storm still howled, the sea was still awful, and night was coming on—another night of horrors—but the Timmons carried her head free, and a feeling akin to confidence was beginning to take place of despair in the breasts of the crew.

They passed in the gloom of the starless night upon that wild waste of waters, clinging to the hope that with the coming of another the storm would pass. And their hope was not in vain Gradually the violence of the wind abated, although the sea leaped frantically, and by the next morning had ceased to be alarming. They looked eagerly for the land, gave more sail, and in a few hours recognized points which assured them that they were off Georgetown, S C. With grateful hearts they steered for the bar and entered the bay in safety, with no other damage to the Timmons than the loss of her boats, sails and rigging, a foremast rubbed almost in two and some strained timbers.

Joe Arnold still lives and pursues his calling, and he will be greatly astonished if he ever sees this account of his heroism, for he is modest and does not think he did anything worth talking about.

BALD HEAD LIGHTHOUSE.

Homeward Bound.

The throbbing engines cease for a while—there is a great calm—the stillness is profound and almost painful in its intensity. Peace gently folds her silent wings, and broods over the placid deep the day is waning, and as we view the majestic grandeur of the scene, our hearts respond to the prophetic vision of the lonely exile on Patmos, who saw beyond the barrier of his mortal life the walls of jasper, and the city of pure gold, where there shall be no more sea.

*   *

The sun is sinking in the Western ocean, bathed in a sea of glory. "The image of Eternity, the throne of the Invisible." Ever changing clouds of silver, of amber, of gold, reflect the beauty of the Better Land, which eye hath not seen, nor the heart of man conceived. "A realm where the rainbow never fades—where the stars are spread out like the islands that slumber on the ocean, and where the beautiful beings who now pass before us like shadows, shall remain forever in our presence."

shadowy river. Weary nature seems to sleep. Our steamer's head is toward the ancient city whose honored name she bears. The anchor lights are gleaming in the harbor--the warning whistle tells us that the time to part has come; like

> "Ships that pass in the night, and speak each other in passing,
> Only a signal shown and a distant voice in the darkness;
> So on the Ocean of Life we pass and speak one another,
> Only a look and a voice, then darkness again and silence."

J. S.

MEN OF THE PAST.

"If a man die shall he live again?" was the inquiry of the Patriarch centuries ago, and inspiration answers in regard to the spiritual and our own knowledge and experience to that of the natural life, and each in the affirmative, for there really is no death. A man's good and great actions survive after he himself has departed, and keep him in continued remembrance, not only by his contemporaries, but by posterity, for his name and the story of his life exists forever and is held up as a beacon light and an example to incite future generations to noble deeds and lofty enterprises. Michael Angelo, Titian, Raphael, and other great masters still live though long since passed away, and speak to us to-day through their works, and the majesty of their deeds in words of "living light;" and they will live forever. And so with others the world over; they are found in every country, and among all peoples, and monuments are erected to commemorate their deeds, and poetry and song embalm their memories in the hearts of a grateful people. There are heroes in every walk in life, even the humblest, and who well deserve the plaudits of the world, but whose names do not appear upon the scroll of fame, whose lives are an example for others, and who have benefited the world by acts of heroism unknown beyond the limits of their own contracted surroundings.

Within the grandest sacred building of the British Kingdom may be seen this inscription upon the tomb of its renowned architect and builder: "Beneath lies Christopher Wren, architect of this church and city, who lived more than ninety years, not for himself but for the public. Reader, do you seek his monument? Look around you!" A modest and unassuming statement, yet how grand and beautiful in its simplicity, and how well intended to excite emotion. He lived not for himself, but for the public, and that noble virtue was illustrated years ago by the people of the then small town of Wilmington to their great detriment, and to the ruin of many, while others have reaped the benefit of their generous and unselfish public spirit. In 1835 it was determined to build the Wilmington & Weldon Railroad, and books were opened for subscription to its stock. The citizens of Wilmington, in their individual capacity, subscribed to a greater amount of the stock than the value of the entire property of the town listed for taxation, an act unprecedented in our history and never equalled so far as is known. They were determined that the road should be built, and it was done; but very many of them beggared themselves in the effort, while others received all the benefit of the sacrifices they had made. It is painful to recall the fact that nearly all the early friends of that great undertaking have passed away and are well-nigh forgotten, and in many cases their very graves are undistinguishable from those of the multitude sleeping around. Is it not a reflection upon our people that neither marble nor bronze should have been erected to mark the spot where their ashes repose?

In the following list are some of the names of the most active friends of that enterprise, who undertook the great work for the public good; also some of the names of others who acted well their part in later years, and deserved a place in the memory of our Wilmington people:

Edward B. Dudley, Governor, and first President of the Wilmington & Weldon Railroad.

James Owen, Member of Congress, and second President of the Wilmington & Weldon Railroad.

Alexander McRae, Civil Engineer and third President of the Wilmington & Weldon Railroad.

P. K. Dickinson, mill owner, successful merchant.

Alexander Anderson, merchant and Mayor of the town.

O. G. Parsley, mill owner and large real estate holder, Bank President, Railroad President, Mayor, and a man of great firmness and integrity.

Asa A. Brown, Editor of the Chronicle.

Aaron Lazarus, prominent merchant.

Thomas H. Wright, Physician and President Bank of Cape Fear.
Wm. B. Meares, Lawyer and Planter and eminent citizen.
E. P. Hall, Merchant and President State National Bank.
J. J. Hill, Physician and Planter.
W. A. Wright, Lawyer, prominent and useful citizen.
Joseph H. Watters, prominent planter and citizen.
John M Rae, Merchant, and first Mayor of Wilmington.
Henry Nutt, Father of the improvements on Cape Fear river, and foremost in public spirit.
Edward Kidder, originator and promoter of Clarendon Water Works, mill owner, and the first to utilize saw dust for fuel, friend of popular education.
Gilbert Potter, mill owner, successful merchant.
James S. Green, first Secretary and Treasurer of the Wilmington & Weldon Railroad until his death, 1862.
W. A. Williams, dry goods merchant.
R. H. Cowan, Sr., planter.
John Wooster, dry goods merchant and turpentine distiller.
Dr. F. McRee, physician, planter and botanist.
James H. Dickson, physician of great attainments.
Z. Latimer, wealthy merchant.
W. J. Harriss, prominent physician.
Christopher Dudley, for many years Post Master of the city.
W. C. Lord, Collector of the Port, sound judgment and great business education.
John Hill, physician, Cashier and President Bank of Cape Fear.
P. W. Boave, a good merchant, and esteemed for his probity.
W. Dunn, merchant, and familiar with all matters of business.
J. W. K. Dix, prominent merchant.
John C. Latta, merchant and Christian gentleman.
Isaac Northrop, large mill owner.
Robert Burr, Jr., distinguished journalist.
James T. Miller, Mayor of the town and Chairman County Court.
E. C. Worth, generous hearted merchant.

Rt. Rev. Bishop Atkinson, Bishop of the Diocese of North Carolina.
Cyrus S. VanAmringe, a gifted young business man.
C. L. Grafflin, incorporator and first Superintendent of Navassa Guano Company.
T. Savage, Cashier Commercial Bank.
E. T. Hancock, merchant of prominence.
H. R. Savage, Cashier Cape Fear Bank.
W. T. Daggett, successful merchant.
Daniel B. Baker, prominent lawyer.
W. M. Parker, merchant and prominent in religious circles.
N. Green Daniel, a thorough merchant and faithful friend.
N. N. Nixon, the largest peanut planter of his day.
Daniel L. Russell, planter and politician.
Eli Murray, merchant, possessing many good traits.
R. H. Cowan, accomplished scholar and orator.
C. D. Myers, inspector and Captain in C. S. A.
John A. Taylor, a public spirited citizen and successful man of business.
Rev. Dr. Drane, the beloved Rector of St. James.
W. A. Berry, physician and scholar.
Dougald McMillan, large and prominent planter.
F. J. Cutlar, physician, and a most estimable gentleman.
Samuel Davis, long associated with our newspapers.
Robert Strange, the able jurist, accomplished scholar and chivalrous gentleman.
W. S. Anderson, jeweller and alderman.
R. S. French, Judge, and ornament of the bar.
Eli W. Hall, a notable citizen and lawyer.
Wm. McRae, Brigadier General, Confederate Army.
S. H. Morton, prominent merchant.
D. R. Murchison, successful merchant, endowed with great boldness and sound judgment.
W. L. Smith, successful insurance agent and Mayor of the City.
Isaac B. Grainger, Bank President of great attainments.

VI

J. L. Hathaway, a prosperous and conservative merchant.
Levi A. Hart, prominent citizen, proprietor Foundry Works.
Thomas L. Colville, inventor, master machinist.
W. H. McRary, a successful merchant.
John C. Bailey, Iron Founder and machinist.
John Dawson, Mayor and merchant.
James Anderson, merchant.
J. C. Walker, a skilful physician and amiable gentleman.
James M. Stevenson, inspector and Captain in C. S. A.
James Dawson, successful banker.
Robert B. Wood, architect, builder and honored citizen.
Geo. R. French, a prosperous merchant and philanthropist.
Frank Brown, active merchant.
Wm. S. Ashe, Member of Congress and President Wilmington & Weldon Railroad.
Robert G. Rankin, prominent merchant, a gallant Captain of Artillery. C. S. A., who fell in the last battle of the war, pierced by three bullets; his garments showed eleven bullet holes.
Rev. Father Murphy, who died at his post during the yellow fever epidemic, beloved by all.
Rev. John L. Pritchard, the faithful pastor and loving friend.
J. A. Engelhard, Editor of Journal and Secretary of State.
Thos. D. Walker, President Wilmington & Manchester Railroad.
Alexander Sprunt, British Vice Consul and merchant.
S. D. Wallace, President Wilmington & Weldon Railroad and Bank Cashier.
W. L. Saunders, Secretary of State and Historian.
Geo. Davis, lawyer, statesman and beloved citizen.
A. L. Price, Founder of the Wilmington Journal.
Edwin E. Burruss, banker, a warm-hearted and genial friend.
R. R. Bridgers, President Wilmington & Weldon and Wilmington, Columbia & Augusta Railroads.
George Chadbourn, mill owner and President National Bank.

John L. Holmes, prominent lawyer.

Donald MacRae, President Navassa Guano Company, and a successful financier.

P. W. Fanning, Grand Master of Masons and sterling citizen.

M. London, a prominent member of the bar.

E. A. Anderson, a skilful physician and an honor to the profession.

A. H. VanBokkelen, the friend of Confederate soldiers, one of our foremost citizens.

Will. Geo. Thomas, an accomplished physician and a prominent citizen.

John C. Heyer, successful merchant and honest man.

Thomas F. Wood, "the beloved physician" and botanist.

Robert E. Calder, one of the noblest of Wilmington's sons.

F. J. Lord, Spanish Vice Consul and an honest man.

Julius A. Bonitz, the progressive editor.

T. D. Love, a gallant Confederate soldier.

B. R. Dunn, Engineer of Roadway, Atlantic Coast Line.

B. F. Mitchell, a most worthy citizen, grain merchant.

L. C. Jones, Superintendent of the Carolina Central Railroad.

O. G. Parsley, Jr., once an active business man, and subsequently Post Master of the City.

Geo. Sloan, Superintendent of the Wilmington Compress and Warehouse Company.

Jos. Price, Harbor Master and gallant soldier.

J. Francis King, prominent physician.

F. W. Potter, physician, and Superintendent of Health.

G. H. Kelly, weigher and inspector.

J. J. Hedrick, merchant, and a brilliant officer of the Confederacy.

Henry Flanner, druggist and soldier.

R. E. Heide, Danish Vice Consul and merchant.

W. P. Elliott, identified with the trade of the Upper Cape Fear.

M. M. Katz, dry goods merchant.

L. B. Huggins, successful merchant.

Wm. G. Fowler, coal merchant.

L. Vollers, merchant.
Edward Savage, a prominent merchant, and afterwards Colonel in the Confederate army.
Thomas J. Southerland, liveryman and Captain in C. S. A.
James F. McRee, Surgeon Confederate States army.
E. S. Tennent, physician, notably allied to our Wilmington people, who fell at Secessionville, S. C., a Confederate soldier.
A. H. Cutts, an experienced and trusted railroad officer.
G. A. Peck, hardware merchant and excellent citizen.
T. F. Toon, Colonel C. S. A., a friend of the sailor.
Hugh Waddell, a notable lawyer and eminent citizen.
James A. Willard, merchant.
F. A. Newbury, merchant.
Robert Morrison, coal dealer.
Alfred A. Moffitt, merchant and a good man.
Will C. Meares, a beloved young man.
W. H. Lippitt, prominent druggist.
Frank Darby, lawyer.
Junius D. Gardner, bank officer.
Alexander Johnson, excellent merchant and citizen.
John Judge, experienced accountant and merchant.
H. B. Eilers, excellent citizen and Christian gentleman.
M. J. DeRosset, Sr., prominent physician.
James Fulton, editor of Journal.
Joshua G. Wright, prominent lawyer.
Thomas Loring, newspaper editor.
J. C. Abbott, General U. S. Army, large mill-owner.
M. J. DeRosset, brilliant scholar and noted physician.
Joshua Walker, physician, amiable gentleman.
William B. Giles, honored and beloved Christian gentleman.
Richard A. Bradley, prominent mill owner.
John Hampden Hill, prominent planter, eminent citizen and physician.
Wm. N. Peden, a prominent citizen for fifty years.

S. M. West, an upright merchant.
Gaston Meares, Colonel C. S. A.
Louis H. DeRosset, a gifted business man.

Joseph S. Murphy, accountant and successful merchant.
John E. Lippitt, successful merchant.

Hugh W. McLaurin, expert accountant, and others whose names are not at this moment remembered.

Among the younger men, who have passed away in recent years, and who had developed in many good traits and bid fair to be classed among the prominent men of our city, we recall L. P. Davis, T. C. DeRosset, J. B. Willard, L. S. F. Brown, John H. Daniel, Edwin A. Northrop, Jas. McR. Cowan, John MacRae, Thos. J. Sinclair, DuVal French, Louis J. Poisson, Norwood Gause, James Elliott, Herbert Perdew, Murray Grant, William Grant.

It may be appropriate and a matter of interest to some to recall in connection with the "Men of the Past" the name of Thomas Godfrey, son of the inventor of the Quadrant and the author of the first dramatic work written in America. He died in this city and was buried in the old graveyard adjoining St. James' Church in August, 1763. While living here he wrote his tragedy "The Prince of Parthia."

x

MEN OF THE PRESENT.

Business, in every age of the world has been the chief pioneer in the march of man's civilization. Blessings everywhere follow its advancing footsteps. It brings humanity into friendly and harmonious intercourse. It removes local prejudices, breaks down personal antipathies and binds the whole family of mankind together by strong ties of association and of mutual and independent interests. It brings men together where towns and cities are built, it leads them to venture upon the high seas in ships and traverse continents on iron pathways, and wherever we go, whether abroad or at home, it is business that controls the great interests of the world, and makes mighty the affairs of men

Wilmington has six lines of railroads: the Wilmington & Weldon Railroad to the North; the Wilmington, Columbia & Augusta Railroad to the South; The Cape Fear and Yadkin Valley Railroad to the West; the Carolina Central Railroad along the Southern tier of Counties in the State to the West; the Wilmington, Newbern & Norfolk Railway along the Eastern tier of Counties in the State to the North; and the Wilmington Sea Coast Railroad to the Atlantic Ocean.

XI

Steamship Line direct to New York, also to Georgetown, S. C.; Steamboat lines on the Cape Fear River to Fayetteville; on Black River to Point Caswell; and on the lower Cape Fear River to Carolina Beach and Southport.

Ocean steamers during the fall, winter and early spring to Liverpool, Bremen and other ports in Europe.

Sailing vessels to the near by rivers, and estuaries; also to all coast-wise and foreign ports when required.

Steam tugs for deep water towing, and harbor and river towing.

EMINENT CITIZENS.

The record of the past and of the present would be incomplete without a grateful reference to the lives of a few of our eminent citizens who, having served long and faithfully their day and generation, have now retired from the activities of a well-spent life and await with Christian calmness and an abiding faith the summons to their reward. Six of them are octogenarians, whose shining examples as Christians, as patriots, as men of affairs, our youth would do well to emulate. We distinguish them by the good they have done in public and private life;

and by their long and faithful devotion to the best interests of our city and commonwealth. When they have passed away may coming generations honor and revere the memory of Mr. John S. James, Dr. A. J. DeRosset, Mr. Alfred Martin, Mr. Alfred Alderman, Dr. John D. Bellamy, Col. James G. Burr and others whose names have long been, and happily are still, household words in Wilmington.

ATLANTIC COAST LINE.

... nt and remarkable of Wilmington industries is that of Atlantic Coast Line Company. The development of ... tion of forces was largely due to the industry, intelli- ... late Mr. W. T. Walters, of Baltimore; and its ... in the face of almost general depression in railway ... rior skill and foresight of its present executive staff, ... Mr. Harry Walters, the only son of its projector.

... stockholders of 1895 was marked by a melancholy ... ation of resolutions of respect to the memory of the ... the greatest of North Carolinians, who, too, alas, was

"The fortunate soldier who makes a wilderness ... be the world's hero, and the theme of its ... are to live when the soldier has passed ... life with a broad charity and an untiring ... places which the soldier has made, ought not ... ated remembrance of those whom his labors have ... in a great measure, is the life history of William T. ... but the incapable of sound discrimination which withholds its commendation, because in benefiting others he also benefited himself. Those of us who remember the country between Charleston and Richmond, when it was first awakened by his touch, and who look upon it now, will need no aid to invoke our grateful remembrance. * * * * * His keen sagacity to discern where great possibilities lay dormant, and the courage to grasp and fix them, the ability to command great resources and to weld and organize them, never losing sight of details until the whole were moulded into one consistent plan, and then the energy and resolution which moved on as resistless as fate, until the work was done—these lifted him up to the level of those merchant princes of old who sat at the board of kings and propped the revenues of empires. He was no gilded youth, dallying with opportunities and catching them only when they fell into his hands. He made his opportunities and utilized them for himself and that after all, was the great lesson of his life."

The system comprises fifteen Southern roads, with an aggregate of 1,540 miles of track, extending from Richmond and Norfolk on the North, to Charleston, Columbia, and Denmark on the South. The company owns and employs 180 locomotives, 3,800 freight cars, and 135 passenger coaches. The number of employes varies between 4,800 and 5,300 men.

The fastest railway journey ever made in the South was completed over the Coast Line in 1894, from Jacksonville to Washington, 780 miles, in fifteen hours and forty-nine minutes, by a special train for the accommodation of the Knights of Pythias. The actual running time was fifty-three miles an hour. This was done via the Wilson Short Cut, "the fly in the amber" from a Wilmington point of view, by which we lose the through connection of former days, and which has probably proved as unprofitable to the Company, as it has been injurious to Wilmington.

Colonel Warren G. Elliott, President of several railroads included in the system, was elected to this most important position on the death of Hon. R. R. Bridgers. Colonel Elliott is a man of broad and liberal views, familiar with the laws governing transportation lines, and thoroughly conversant with the administrative department. He is admired for his genial and social qualities as well as for his bright intellect and business knowledge.

XIV

Probably no other stranger who ever cast his lot in Wilmington has gained so quickly and so generally the friendship, esteem and cordial good-will of our people.

Major J. R. Kenly's reputation as Manager of this great system extends beyond the sea. Endowed with an active and discerning mind, he readily comprehends the most difficult problems and with rapidity arrives at conclusions. From the minutest details he is familiar with all that pertains to executive control of the myriads of forces which play their parts in this grand aggregation. Secure in the assurance of his power to wield and weld this force into a harmonious whole and to direct the whole for the best interest of his system, he impresses everyone strongly with his thoughtful, serious face and courteous demeanor, which so often characterize the man who is born to lead in the great business of life.

Captain John F. Divine, General Superintendent, one of the oldest officials of the line, has ever been faithful and devoted to the interests of the companies he has served for so many years. His long experience has given him a thorough knowledge of the requirements for successfully and economically operating railroads. He has long enjoyed the reputation of being better informed as to the cost of construction and equipment than any one in the South. Captain Divine is one of our most esteemed citizens, kind and considerate, charitable and benevolent, and always willing to lend a helping hand in the up-building of his city and State.

Mr. W. A. Riach, the General Auditor, has long experience in his profession. A gentleman of education and refinement, an expert accountant, trained under the most favorable conditions in his native Scotland, he retains the confidence and esteem of not only the great corporation which he so ably represents but of our entire community.

His superior traits of heart and mind in works of Christian benevolence have been recognized and honored by our best people.

The enormous increase in the freight business of this system has been developed under the able management of the Traffic Manager, Mr. T. M. Emerson, who brought to this field the skill and experience of a well-trained and forceful mind. Nothing short of a genius in railroad affairs could have held the lead in Southern traffic management that Mr. Emerson has sustained for five years past. Always alert, with an intellectual penetration not excelled in his profession, this Argus of the hundred eyes suffers nothing to escape him that would under his skilful direction subserve the interest of his employers. His tranquil countenance never betrays the workings of his well-balanced mind, and any one who tries to surprise his confidence in an attempt to cut rates, will soon find it a hopeless task.

Mr. Horace M. Emerson, Assistant General Freight and Passenger Agent, is steadily buiding a reputation which is already second to none in his line of duty. Affable, courteous, persuasive, he exemplifies superior tact, which, with a tenacity of purpose, effects results simply unattainable by heroic measures.

Mr. James F. Post, Jr., Treasurer, has a thorough knowledge of the intricate and voluminous transactions which give life and strength to large corporations, and that he has performed his duties acceptably is well attested by his ability to give general satisfaction. His promotion from a subordinate place to the responsible position he now fills, reflects credit on his financial knowledge and capabilities. He takes great interest in education, and for many years has served as Chairman of School District No. 1. He has served as Alderman, and is active in city affairs. And last, but not least, is a faithful and consistent member of the Methodist Church, having served his people as Superintendent of the Sunday School. Mr. Post is generally liked by his associates and friends.

Mr. E. Borden, Superintendent of Transportation, is eminently fitted for the place. The variety and completeness of his work, the methods of its arrangement, the necessary orders and instructions to guide, command our respect and admiration. He might be termed a specialist in his branch of railroading, having given more attention to this particular line, and this enables him to lend a helping hand to those occupying other positions, dependent on his prompt movement of trains. He has been wonderfully successful, and stands high with his Company. Mr. Borden is quiet and unassuming and possessed of many superior traits of character.

THE CHAMPION COMPRESSES AND WAREHOUSES.

XVII

ALEXANDER SPRUNT & SON.

The Champion Compress and Warehouse Company's plant adjoins to that of the Atlantic Coast Line. This corporation was chartered by the State of North Carolina in 1879, and the entire capital stock is owned by the proprietors, who have long controlled it and whose export business alone has fostered and sustained it.

The property includes 420,000 square feet of warehouse and dock space, with storage capacity of twenty thousand bales of cotton. Two of the largest Morse Compressors of ninety inch cylinders, are kept going from the beginning to the end of the cotton season. Their capacity is 3,000 bales in twenty-four hours, and more than a million bales of cotton have been pressed by them during the past fifteen years, with scarcely a break of serious consequence. The plant is said to be the most convenient and complete of its kind in the United States. The warehouses are protected from fire by a thorough system of automatic sprinklers, which have never failed in any emergency. The proprietors, Alexander Sprunt & Son, were the pioneers of the steam foreign trade in Wilmington, having previous to the charter of their first steamer, "Barnesmore," in 1881, been largely engaged in the naval stores trade, by sailing craft, and their business kept steady pace with the development of navigation by river and harbor improvement under the direction of United States Engineers. The "Barnesmore's" draft was 13 feet and her cargo 3,458 bales of cotton. The "Jeanara" took last year 11,250 bales of cotton on 18½ feet of water. The firm has frequently loaded as many as five large steamers simultaneously, and the present class of boats employed by them average a capacity of 10,000 bales. The firm's direct agencies extend from Barcelona and Genoa, on the Mediterranean, in the South, to Helsingfors, in the Gulf of Finland, and Moscow, in central Russia, in the North of Europe. They have also an office and staff in Liverpool and in Ghent.

XVIII

"THE ORTON."

...nd ...ttractions of Wilmington, North Carolina, as a
... ... widely recognized every year. Its location,
... ... Coast Line, only eighteen hours from New York,
... ...sting place for both Northbound and Southbound
... ... way between Jacksonville and New York City.
... W...ngton is excellent; there is not a more healthful
... ... States. "The Orton" is one of the best Hotels

ORTON PLANTATION—FRONT VIEW.

ORTON RICE FIELD.

COLONIAL ROAD AT ORTON.

ORTON HOMESTEAD.

in the South—containing all modern comforts and conveniences, including excellent beds, dainty, well-prepared food, electric lights, Otis elevator and return call-bell system.

This establishment was built and is owned by a prominent North Carolinian, a resident of New York, who has sustained robust health and fine spirits by a Winter residence near Wilmington on his historic Colonial plantation, Orton, where he keeps a well-stocked game preserve.

The table of "The Orton" Hotel in Wilmington is supplied with rice-fed poultry from this old farm, which in flavor and tenderness cannot be equaled at any other hostelry North or South.

WORTH & WORTH.

This well-known firm was established by Dr. T. C. Worth, who came to Wilmington in 1852, and conducted successfully a large shipping business. He was joined in 1853 by his brother, B. G. Worth, Esq., and the firm style changed to T. C. & B. G. Worth. At that time all merchandise from the North for the interior of this State, and also for a part of South Carolina and Tennessee was brought by fast sailing packets from Philadelphia, New York, Boston and Baltimore to Wilmington, and transhipped in part by rail, but mostly by river steamboats to the country. An immense business was done by forwarding merchants here, who charged 20 per cent on the freight for their service, and the wharves of Wilmington were lined for a mile or more with the beautiful white-winged schooners, sometimes two or three abreast. River property was valuable in those days, as the following incident will show: A small wharf below Market street, which would not realize more than two hundred dollars a year now, was being rented at public auction, and the veteran crier, Mr. M. Cronly, surprised by the lively competition of responsible bidders, which reached sixteen hundred dollars, came to a full stop and said: "Gentlemen, please understand that I am not SELLING this wharf, I am only renting it for one year!"

XXII

Messrs. T. C. & B. G. Worth were also largely interested in the river steamboats plying between Wilmington and Fayetteville, and were agents of the Cape Fear Steamboat Company. The Worths built the "Flora McDonald," "A. P. Hurt" and "Governor Worth." The "Hurt" still survives. We recall the names of a few of the sailing vessels regularly engaged in our trade at that time: "Damon," "Charles E. Thorn," "Alfred F. Thorn," "Repeater," "Regulus," "Aloric," "Venus," "DeRosset," "John," "Ned," "Ben," "Alba," "Mary Powell," "A. D ke," "Belle," "David Duffield," "Myrover," "Lilly," "David Faust," "Wm. L. Springs," "E. S. Powell," "Enchantress." There was also quite a fleet of small sailing craft styled "corn crackers," which brought corn in bulk and in bags from the Eastern counties, Hyde county being the chief. Three of these sprightly little schooners bore peculiar, and at times when off their schedules, strangely inappropriate names: "We'r Here," "I'm Coming," "So Am I".

In 1872 Dr. T. C. Worth died, and after several changes of the firm name it became Worth & Worth, the present partners being Messrs. B. G. Worth, D. G. Worth and C. W. Worth. The house has always ranked high in the commercial ratings of Wilmington, and its members are prominent in public and social life, especially and notably so in their liberal support of the cause of Christian benevolence.

The writer, who received his early training from one of the leaders of business affairs in Wilmington, Mr. David G. Worth, would fain pay his tribute in this connection to the virtues and excellence of his former employer. The records of Wilmington do not contain a more patriotic citizen, a more upright merchant, a more consecrated life, a more devoted friend, than David Gaston Worth. In early youth he acquired from his distinguished father the late Governor Jonathan Worth—those traits of heart and mind which, fitly joined together, make up the life and character of the gracious Christian gentleman. Of remarkable intellectual endowment and superior business penetration, he daily illustrates with character, modesty, a broad charity and a noble purpose which our young men would do well to emulate.

THE CLYDE STEAMSHIP COMPANY.

Adjoining the Champion Compress and Warehouse Company's dock is the wharf of the Clyde Steamship Company. Their steamers run between New York and Wilmington, N. C., and Georgetown, S. C., bringing large quantities of freight South for Wilmington and the interior, and taking lumber, cotton, naval stores and many other products to New York, Canada, Northwest and points in Europe. The steamers consist of Steamship "George W. Clyde," 1574 tons; Steamship "Delaware," 1272 tons; Steamship "Pawnee," 858 tons; Steamship "Croatan," 827 tons; Steamship "Oneida," 752 tons, forming a fleet of fast, able steamers, with good passenger accommodation. General office is at 5 Bowling Green, New York, and the Traffic Manager of the line is Mr. Theo. G. Eger. The company is ably represented here by Mr. H. G. Smallbones, as Superintendent, who has been long and favorably known in Wilmington.

THE WILMINGTON COTTON MILLS.

The Wilmington Cotton Mills was incorporated in the year 1874. It has been operated continuously since that time, first as a Print Cloth mill, and later, with the addition of a dye-house and finishing machinery, the production was so changed as to include a wide range of fabrics, such as crasher, gingham, cotton worsted and domestics.

At the present time the mill is making domestics and napped goods almost exclusively. The product is sold in the North and Northwest, in the principal markets, and to the largest buyers in the country, thus meeting successfully severe competition and demonstrating the fact that in Wilmington there are no serious obstacles to continued expansion of textile industries.

The mill employs about two hundred people, and pays to employes about $4,000 per month; uses 2,000 bales of cotton a year; runs 7,000 spindles, 286 looms and dyeing and finishing machinery.

XXIV

...n achinery was added during 1894 and 1895, and during 1896
...ilding has been completed, which will add greatly to the
... the plant and to its efficiency. Plans are now being made
...g the dyeing and finishing departments.
...rs of the corporation are: President, Hugh MacRae; Vice
... David G. Worth; Secretary and Treasurer, Donald MacRae;
...nt, J. W. Hawkins; Directors—Matt J. Heyer, B. G. Worth,
... D. G. Worth, D. MacRae and Hugh MacRae.

PATTERSON, DOWNING & CO.

... a] the most extensive house in the naval stores trade in the
... Their business connections extend throughout the great
... Canada, and their foreign agencies are in every port abroad
... and turpentine demand justifies the expense. They have
... New York, Wilmington, Charleston, Savannah, Bruns-
... ably in other places.
... managed in New York by a former Wilmingtonian, Mr. E. S.
... nt here is his brother, Mr. H. K. Nash.
... been long and favorably known as a merchant and
... ability and a gentleman of extraordinary social

J. H. SLOAN. COTTON BUYER.

... business in Charlotte and has an agency in Wilmington
... charge of Mr. A. H. Brenner.
... member of the late firm of Walker, Fleming & Sloan,
... experience in the trade.
... foreign steamers in their cotton export trade from
... abroad and represents the well-known cotton mer-
... McLaren & Bro., of Philadelphia.

XXV

THE SEABOARD AIR LINE.

Controlling over one thousand miles of railway, and having one of its termini in the city of Wilmington, has been one of the principal factors in promoting the prosperity of the city. The Carolina Central Railway Company, constituting that part of the Seaboard Air Line which reaches Wilmington, succeeded the Wilmington, Charlotte & Rutherford Railroad Company, which was projected and partly constructed prior to the war. It traverses the prosperous and fertile tier of counties on the Southern border of the State, and has a length of 287 miles, extending to the foot of the Blue Ridge Mountains. It is intersected 110 miles west of Wilmington by the main line of the System, the latter reaching from Portsmouth to Atlanta and placing our city in easy reach of both the North and the South.

First-class passenger service, with quick schedules, is operated, and all Southern, Western and Northwestern points are easy of access to travellers. This is also the case as to Northern and Western cities. A large number of visitors, some for short stay, and some spending the summer, come from the interior for the benefit of the salt water bathing, the good service affording a comfortable trip from Georgia, Alabama and other Southern States. Transfers to trains to the beach or boat for the river to Southport are made without expense, and without trouble.

A large freight business is handled in and out of Wilmington, both local and to distant points. Excellent freight connections guarantee prompt movement, and the consolidation of the several roads now comprising the System under one general management, has given Wilmington a fast and serviceable route to and from all the great markets of the North and West.

Attention is especially called, however, to the strenuous efforts being made by the Seaboard Air Line towards advertising the resources of the South, in the benefits of which Wilmington will share in proportion to its endeavors in the same direction. Mr. E. St. John, Vice-President and General Manager, became convinced immediately after assuming charge of the Line, a little over a year ago, that the prosperity of the Southern

...try and consequently of the railroads traversing it, was largely dependent upon augmenting its populace with the same class of industrious, thrifty and intelligent farmers by whom the West had been built up, and he organized a special department under his immediate direction, in the interests of immigration. Thorough knowledge of the wants to be supplied and a wide experience in the management of a large system of railroad in the West, outlined a policy which is beginning to bear fruit, and promises to build up the waste places in the South, putting in cultivation the fertile fields now idle, which should be yielding abundant harvests. A publication in the interest of intending settlers is published monthly, and can be had free of charge from any agent. In addition a handsome, illustrated pamphlet, with carefully prepared description of the lands along the Line can be had by addressing (with four cents for postage) Mr. George L. Rhodes, General Agent, Portsmouth, Virginia, who gives this department his personal supervision.

The interests of the Seaboard Air-Line at Wilmington are in charge of Mr. Thomas D. Meares, General Agent. The offices of the line are in Portsmouth Va., the following being a list of the general officers:

J. St. John, Vice-President and General Manager; V. E. McBee, General Superintendent; H. W. B. Glover, Traffic Manager; Geo. L. Rhodes, General Agent; Charles R. Capps, General Freight Agent; T. J. Anderson, General Passenger Agent.

Mr. Thomas D. Meares, the Wilmington Agent, is a conspicuous representative of an old and honored family of the Cape Fear. His fine courtesy, his frank and manly qualities and his recognized business ability have won him many friends in social, political and professional life. Elected an Alderman of the city some years ago, his official acts have been marked by singleness of purpose—the promotion of the public good. He believes in the benefits of advertising, and has already accomplished much by that means for the development of Eastern North Carolina and for the Road which he so ably represents.

XXVII

NAVASSA GUANO COMPANY OF WILMINGTON.

As early as 1804, Humboldt had described deposits of guano on the Islands of the Pacific ocean off the coast of Peru. The increasing demand and large exportation of this article from these Islands stimulated search for new localities, and in 1856 deposits were discovered in the West Indies, including the Island of Navassa. This Island was purchased by a party of enterprising Americans and placed under the protectorate of the United States Government, and has the distinction of being the only foreign possession of this Government outside of Alaska. Immediately upon obtaining possession of this Island the projectors cast around for a suitable location for the establishment of a plant to utilize the valuable deposits found there, and Wilmington was selected as the most available point in the South for the distribution of their manufactured product.

On the 5th day of August, 1869, letters patent were issued by Governor Holden, of North Carolina, to Robert R. Bridgers, George W. Grafflin and Francis W. Kerchner, creating them a body politic and corporate to be known as Navassa Guano Company of Wilmington, for the purpose of manufacturing fertilizers and chemicals, mining and working the necessary ores, and such other things as may be incident to the manufacture and sale of fertilizers and chemicals. This Company was promptly organized, its capital stock subscribed for, officers elected and a site, known as Meares' Bluff, on the Cape Fear river, about four miles above Wilmington, secured. The erection of their plant was rapidly pushed forward, and as soon as practicable the Company began the work of manufacturing commercial fertilizers. The Navassa Guano Company has developed into one of the largest and most successful organizations engaged in this important industry, and is to-day one of the best known industrial enterprises ever originated in the South, attesting the foresight of the gentlemen who conceived this idea. This plant was established and in successful operation long before the deposits of phosphate were known or exploited around Charleston, and before a single factory had been established at that centre.

The plant is well located, being situated on the banks of the Cape Fear river, where vessels from all parts of the world can proceed to discharge th... cargoes of materials; in addition, they have most excellent terminal ... connecting all the important railroads which centre at Wilmington. Th... procure their material from all parts of the United States, and ... from South America, the West Indies, Italy and Germany. Their ... thoroughly equipped with all modern devices and appliances for ... manufacture of high grade fertilizers, and their enormous w... occupy something over six acres of floor space.

The Navassa Guano Company claims the distinction of being the pioneer fertilizer industry in the South, which, since the establishment of ... has developed into enormous proportions, giving employment ... thousands of people, utilizing thousands of tons of what was formerly ... and representing an investment of about $40,000,000.

THE WILMINGTON, NEWBERN AND NORFOLK RAILWAY.

The Wilmington, Newbern and Norfolk Railway was completed and in operation between Wilmington and Jacksonville, North Carolina, a distance of fifty miles, by February 1st, 1891, under the charter of the Wilmington, Onslow and East Carolina Railroad. Subsequently it was extended thirty-eight miles northward from Jacksonville to Newbern, namely, under the name of the East Carolina Land and Railway Company; which extension was completed in the latter part of July, 1893. Under legislative authority the two were consolidated by purchase of the East Carolina Land and Railway Company's Railroad, franchises, etc.; and the entire line is, and has been since February, 1894, owned and operated by the Wilmington, Newbern and Norfolk Railway Company.

The railway is of standard gauge, 4′ 9″, namely, and is laid with 56-pound steel rails. The Company has four locomotives, eight passenger cars, three

XXIX

baggage cars and sixty-four freight cars. It also operates a steamer on New River between Jacksonville and Marines, a distance of eighteen miles, the latter point being within about three miles of the mouth of the river. Semi-weekly trips are also made by this steamer to Tar Landing, about seven miles north of Jacksonville, on New River.

In addition to the shipping facilities afforded by the Company at Jacksonville, it has also constructed wharves on New River at Glenoe Stock Farm, seven miles below Jacksonville, and at Moore's Landing, on the west bank, and Marines, on the east bank of New River, eighteen miles below Jacksonville.

At Jacksonville it has numerous sidings running into the property of the Parmele-Eccleston Lumber Company, one of the largest and most completely equipped lumber-milling establishments in the South.

At Newbern the Company has a large and commodious wharf and warehouse on the Neuse River at its Newbern terminal, and an attractive and roomy passenger station and warehouse.

At Wilmington the Wilmington, Newbern and Norfolk Railway Company has a fine terminal property on the Cape Fear River at the south end of the city, on which is a wharf five hundred feet in length along the river, with a depth of water varying at mean low tide from $12\frac{1}{4}$ feet at the extreme northern end of the wharf to 17 feet at the southern end. At this wharf vessels of large tonnage can load and unload directly from the cars and the Company's tracks alongside the wharf, which tracks are capable of holding fourteen freight cars suitably placed for discharging or receiving cargo to and from vessels.

At Surry and Wooster streets, just above the Wilmington Cotton Mills, this railway has another warehouse and operates a valuable wharf property, now occupied, in part, by the United States River and Harbor Improvements Department under a lease. The Company has also leased for forty years the freight line of the Wilmington Street Railway Company, operated by steam dummy along the water-front on the Cape Fear River, and connecting the Wilmington, Newbern and Norfolk Railway on the south with the Cape Fear and Yadkin Valley, the Wilmington, Columbia and Augusta

road, the Wilmington and Weldon Railroad, and the Carolina Central
road, near the extreme north end of the city.
 general offices of the Wilmington, Newbern and Norfolk Railway
 the foot of Orange street, in the Power House of the Wilmington
 Railway. Its principal passenger station and warehouse in town are
 corner of Mulberry and Water streets. Its roundhouse is at Kidder
 in the south end of the city.
 property of this railway company is in all particulars well con-
 ted and equipped. At Newbern it connects with the East Carolina
 atch, thus giving it a through line connection with Norfolk, Baltimore,
 adelphia, New York and other Northern cities.
 is railway is almost entirely owned by Mr. Thomas A. McIntyre, of
 m of McIntyre & Wardwell, Produce Exchange, New York City, who
 President The other officers of the Company are: Vice-President
 General Manager, H. A. Whiting, of Wilmington, North Carolina;
 Manager and Auditor, J. W. Martenis, of Wilmington; Treasurer,
 ar A Nash, President Corn Exchange Bank, New York City; Secre-
 C. M Whitlock, of Wilmington; Cashier and Purchasing Agent,
 Howell, Jr., of Wilmington; Engineer of Roadway, W. G. Furlong,
 Wilmington; Master Mechanic, George E. Branch, of Wilmington.

ROBINSON & KING.

 s well known and strictly reliable firm has long been identified with the
 stores trade of Wilmington. The senior member has served repeatedly
 resident of the Produce Exchange, and is thoroughly conversant with
 he details of his business. Consignments from the interior will receive
 ot personal attention. Orders from the North and West and from
 d, could not be placed in better hands. They make a specialty of the

XXXI

BONEY & HARPER.

This firm, the largest in the grain and feed trade of Wilmington, was established by Mr. G. J. Boney in 1884; two years later he associated with him Captain J. T. Harper, who was previously engaged in the steamboat business. The firm possess ample means, and valuable modern machinery, with all needful appliances in the manufacture of hominy and corn meal, which are their principal staples. The capacity of their mills is about two thousand bushels per day. They hold an extensive trade with North and South Carolina, and their well-earned reputation for fair dealing has been established throughout that district. The senior partner was elected President of the Produce Exchange twice, and is one of the most active and intelligent traders of Wilmington. His public acts in political and business life have been rewarded by the recognition and respect of our entire community.

Captain Harper, the junior partner, has established for his own account in Southport, one of the most complete general stores in the State. It is regarded as a model in its various modern appliances for convenience and comfort.

WILMINGTON COMPRESS AND WAREHOUSE COMPANY.

The Wilmington Compress and Warehouse Company was organized in 1874. Operations were immediately commenced with a small Baldwin Press on the present site of the Wilmington, Columbia & Augusta Railroad freight warehouse. The following year a change was made to the present location, north of the Carolina Central Railroad, where the capacity of the plant was increased by the erection of a Tyler Compress. Unfortunately, during the season of 1876, the Baldwin Press broke down, at which time there were twenty-eight vessels in port, loading and waiting for cargoes of cotton. In

1--- the Company was chartered, the Tyler Press was sold, improvements made and a more powerful Hydraulic Compress purchased. Recently another Compress of same make has been added.

The plant now consists of two Compresses, five separate warehouses for the storage of cotton, divided by brick walls into compartments, with a storage capacity of 10,000 bales of cotton and a wharf-front of over a thousand feet, and a depth of water sufficient for the largest steamers coming to the port.

The officers are H. G. Smallbones, President; Walter Smallbones, Secretary and Treasurer.

ATLANTIC NATIONAL BANK.

The Atlantic National Bank was organized in April, 1892, the last installment of the capital stock being paid during October of the same year. This bank does not pay interest on its deposits. Since the first year has paid semi-annual dividends of three per cent., and has increased its surplus account each year, having now a surplus of some $50,000 undivided profits.

The President says: "Those who organized the Atlantic Bank determined to pay no interest on deposits, and to do business only on security as far as possible. As the patrons of Wilmington banks had not been accustomed to seeing banks conducted in this way, the business of the bank was very small to begin with, but the volume of business increased steadily and at the end of the first year the bank had accumulated profits at the rate of about twelve per cent. per annum of the capital employed. Its stock will readily sell at about thirty per cent. premium, though it pays only six per cent. per annum in dividends, besides paying all taxes. The bank makes a specialty of always being able and willing to supply all customers with money at the bottom rates on approved security." This institution employes twelve salaried officers and clerks. J. W. Norwood is President and W. J. Toomer

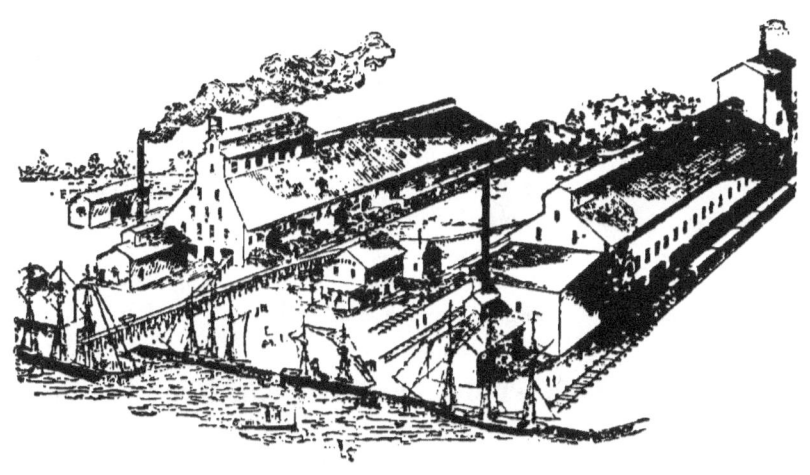

POWERS, GIBBS & CO'S FERTILIZER FACTORY.

POWERS, GIBBS & CO.

Located at Almont, on the North East River, within sight of Wilmington, is the extensive Fertilizer Works of Powers, Gibbs & Co. The plant is fully equipped, with a capacity of 25,000 tons per annum, the product being high grade fertilizers. The capital employed in the business is $200,000.

Mr. Powers, the Wilmington managing partner, has established a large business and sustains it with characteristic skill and energy. His employment of many laborers contributes much to the material prosperity of Wilmington.

MURCHISON & CO.

The firm of Murchison & Co., Bankers, receives money on deposit, subject to check, discounts business paper for depositors, and does a very large collection business. Their facilities for banking in all departments are unsurpassed. The principals have been identified with Wilmington for more than forty years, and they are rated in wealth at one million dollars and upwards. Confidence, caution and conservatism has been the rule of their business life.

The junior partner and Wilmington manager, Mr. Henry C. McQueen, has been long bred to the business of this widely-known firm. He is endowed with a well-balanced judicial mind and versed in all branches of business. He was selected years ago as a member of the Board of Audit and Finance and still holds that honorable position in the municipal government. He has also served as President of the Wilmington Produce Exchange, and is known to our community as an honest Christian gentleman.

THE WILMINGTON STREET RAILWAY CO.

The Wilmington Street Railway Company was incorporated under an act of the General Assembly of North Carolina, February 10th, 1887, and by an amendment in 1891 it was allowed to use electricity as a motive power in place of horses, and was also empowered to sell electric current for the production of arc and incandescent lights for power and heat and for such commercial and other purposes as might be found profitable or desirable.

The electric system of the Wilmington Street Railway Company was put into operation early in 1892. The Company possesses also an exclusive franchise upon especially favorable terms.

In January, 1896, an additional line of track was laid connecting its Castle street branch on the south along 6th, Orange and 9th streets, with the Princess street branch north of the centre of the city; thus forming a complete loop. Its railway property, therefore, embraces at present about 5 miles of track in its passenger line completely equipped with electric motive power; it also owns a freight line 1¼ miles in length most advantageously located along the water-front of the Cape Fear River; which line is well constructed with 60-pound steel T-rails, and is operated by a steam engine. This freight line connects all the steam railways which centre in Wilmington, viz: the Wilmington and Weldon Railroad, the Wilmington, Columbia and Augusta Railroad, these two constituting a part of the Atlantic Coast Line system; the Carolina Central Railroad, forming a part of the Seaboard Air Line system; the Cape Fear and Yadkin Valley Railway, and the Wilmington, Newbern and Norfolk Railway; between these several roads the freight line of the Wilmington Street Railway Company is used to transfer passengers, cars and freight. This freight line has recently been leased to the Wilmington, Newbern and Norfolk Railway Company for a term of forty years upon advantageous terms.

The Company's power house is situated at the corner of Orange and Water streets on the river-front; it is a commodious, two-story brick building, equipped with electric generating apparatus of considerably more than the capacity required at present. All parts of the building and car-sheds are protected by an automatic sprinkler system. The Company also owns a wharf on the Cape Fear River at the foot of Orange street, from which vessels can be loaded directly and unloaded from and into cars.

The officers of the Company at present are as follows: President, H. A. Whiting, Wilmington, North Carolina; Vice-President, B. F. O'Connor, New York City; General Manager, M. F. H. Gouverneur, Wilmington, North Carolina; Secretary and Treasurer, J. W. Martenis, Wilmington, North Carolina.

J. C. STEVENSON & TAYLOR.

The above firm is a native product, both having been born in New Hanover county. The senior received his education in the common schools before the late war, and the junior since the war. The senior was in business for many years as a retailer, and was at one time the proprietor of four establishments, retail groceries, the junior a clerk at that time. At the age of 22 Mr. Taylor was admitted to a partnership, which was about ten years ago, since which time all of the retail stores have been sold

XXXVI

t.. ...sm..ss has gradually gravitated towards an exclusive
...sn.ess, which now extends over nearly every county in the
N..th Car.lin. an.l a large number of counties in South Carolina.
now r..prescnted on the road by five travelling salesmen, and are
...h with the trade, and have superior facilities for handling a
..me .f business. Their quarters are in the central part of the
..nd..g entirely through the block from Front to Water street,
.r h..use on the riverside, where they receive from the boats and
..l.l..ated "Cape Fear" brand of mullets, so popular throughout
T..ey are classed among the largest dealers in molasses in the
.. ke.p c.nstantly on hand a large stock of all grades of molasses
..
g..ntle.r.en, having worked up from the retail trade, are capable of
..l. .ome advice as to how to buy a stock, what to buy, what not
..d .re well versed in the science of trade-winning.

McNAIR & PEARSALL.

. .. .. b..ness .n July, 1888. They are strictly wholesale
.n .. .,. p.. ..t.. of coffee, rice, molasses and salt; although they
. . . .t.. everything kept in an establishment o.th.. kind,
..g..t .. .. King Powder Company, of Cincinnati, Ohio. They
.n t.. C. ... business for the sale of cotton and naval stores.

HILTON LUMBER CO.

... L..b.. C.mpany manufactures rough and dressed lumber,
.. l.t.. .nd shingles from the North Carolina pine and cypress,
.p..s b.. th. most improved mills, with four large dry kilns, five
m..h..t.. .nd one shingle machine. Some 70 hands are employed
...tly .. t.. ..llion feet of lumber a year.

D. L. GORE.

D. L. Gore is a wholesale grocer and commission merchant, and has an extensive trade with the merchants and farmers in the adjoining counties of North and South Carolina. He is also a large dealer in pea-nuts, shipping in quantities to Southern and Western States.

His remarkable success, achieved by habits of thrift, economy and never-failing energy, proves him to be a man of superior ability. He is reckoned among the wealthy merchants of Wilmington.

J. A. SPRINGER & CO.

J. A. Springer & Co., wholesale and retail dealers in coal for domestic, steam, foundry and blacksmithing purposes, established this business in 1873. The retail yards for supplying the city trade are located on Water street near the foot of Chestnut street. The wholesale depot is at the Seaboard Air Line yards, where large stocks of Anthracite coal are handled for rail shipments to interior points in North Carolina, South Carolina and Georgia. All the coal is brought from Philadelphia and New York by vessels and discharged directly into bins and oftentimes direct into cars for through shipment. Special attention is given to coaling steamships with the celebrated Pocahontas coal received direct from the mines by rail.

R. W. HICKS.

The well-known house of R. W. Hicks, wholesale grocer and commission merchant, has been in existence for fifteen years; for ten years previous Mr. Hicks was with Messrs. E. Murray & Co. He carries a full line of groceries and his business amounts to several hundreds of thousand dollars a year. The building he occupies is well adapted to his business, containing more floor space than any other in the city in the same line of trade. He invites all friends to call when visiting the city, whether on business or pleasure.

ROGER MOORE.

Roger Moore's place of business is in the three story brick store, 104 North Water Street, Wilmington, N. C., and warehouse nearly in rear of same, with wharves in front for storage of brick, shingles, laths, etc. He manufactures brick largely, and has always on hand for sale, besides a large stock of his own make, re-pressed brick for fronts, round cornered brick, for windows, doors, etc. He also deals largely in fire brick, clay, best brand of Lime, (Medal), best brand Rosindale "Hoffman" Cement, best brand of Portland Cement—Stettiner his leading brand. Laths, shingles, sawed Cypress and riven Cypress, 4, 5 and 6 inches wide; Longman & Martinez prepared Paints, Oils, &c. Roofing Felt, Sheathing Paper, M. B. Coating Paint for Roofs, Nails, Caps, etc. Aluminite, one of the best wall plasters known; Muresco, of delicate tints, for finishing walls, and a most durable substitute for white-washing at a low price. Also Agricultural Lime and Land Plasters.

S. P. McNAIR.

In 1881, Mr. S. P. McNair came to Wilmington and established himself in the wholesale grocery and general commission business. The success of his undertaking has been marked from the beginning, and his house is well and favorably known throughout the territory in which he operates. He possesses superior facilities for handling consignments, being a member of all exchanges where fluctuations of markets are recorded; thus keeping abreast with the times, he can dispose of the same to advantage.

B. F. KEITH COMPANY.

The B. F. Keith Company are not only wholesale grocers and commission merchants, but are also manufacturers of Colly Mill water-ground meal and shingles. This Company deals in flour, molasses, rice, sugar, coffee, salt fish, tobacco and pea-nuts. Their trade in groceries extends through North Carolina and a part of South Carolina. Their shingle trade is with the West India Islands.

SEAMEN'S FRIEND SOCIETY BUILDING.

SEAMEN'S FRIEND SOCIETY.

This Society was organized fifty-three years ago for the purpose of improving the social, moral and religious condition of seamen. As a means to secure these ends, there has been erected on Front and Dock streets a Seamen's Home and a Seamen's Bethel, where seamen are properly cared for and attended, and where the ministrations of the Gospel can be secured. Services are conducted at the Bethel every Sunday afternoon commencing at 3 o'clock.

Any person contributing Two Dollars annually is a member of the Society, or by paying Twenty Dollars at any one time is a member for life. The officers of the Society are: George Harriss, President; George R. French, Vice-President; W. J. Woodward, Secretary and Treasurer; and the Directors, James Sprunt, John Cowan and Rev. Dr. Robert Strange.

VOLLERS & HASHAGEN.

...ers & Hashagen are engaged in the brokerage and commission business, ...isions, flour and grain. Being provision-packers and millers agents, ... ls are received in car-load lots and disposed to jobbers under the favorable advantages. Having trackage room and their warehouses ... close proximity with the tracks of the Atlantic Coast Line, there ...ving of the expense in drayage or storage. For years they have repre- ... Messrs. Armour, of Chicago, for the sale of their goods at this point, ... handle on commission flour from the Michigan Mills, which is ... of the best grades of flour on the market.

CLARENDON WATER WORKS.

Clarendon Water Works, located at Hilton, were built in 1880–'81, at ... There are three Worthington pumps, with a daily ... 2,000,000 gallons, the system pumping to stand-pipe and direct ... The fire pressure is 100 pounds. There are one hundred ... hydrants, fourteen and one-half miles mains. The source ... Fear river, which Professor Nichols, of Boston Institute of ... a more potable water than is usually furnished ... The rates charged are comparatively low, both for ... and eating purposes.

WILLIAMS, RANKIN & CO.

... Williams, Rankin & Co., wholesale grocers and commission ... and 18 North Water street, are successors of the long-... well known firm of Williams & Murchison. Their facil-... excellent and their correspondence extensive. Mr. ... trained wholesale grocers in Wilmington, and ... work. He never takes a holiday, and if ample ... count for anything, this firm should do a thriving

PEREGOY--JENKINS CO.

The Peregoy-Jenkins Company, a corporation existing by special act of the Legislature of North Carolina, succeeded the Peregoy Lumber Co. August 1st, 1895. This Company manufactures and dresses into flooring, ceiling, partition, siding, casings, mouldings, etc., etc., from twelve to fifteen million feet of North Carolina pine and cypress per annum. Besides, they have capacity for making about six million sawed cypress shingles. Their plant is equipped with all the latest improved machinery, and consists of band saw mill, planing mill and dry kilns. Everything is up to date, well arranged and strongly constructed. They have a large frontage on deep water, the largest vessel having no difficulty in reaching their dock, and ample side-tracks from the railroads terminating at Wilmington. About 100 hands are employed. W. Edwin Peregoy is President and Treasurer, and J. Wilcox Jenkins Secretary.

WILMINGTON SAVINGS AND TRUST COMPANY.

The Wilmington Savings and Trust Company was organized January, 1888. The most prominent promoters were Messrs. H. Walters, D. O'Connor, J. W. Atkinson, B. F. Hall, F. Rheinstein, Pembroke Jones and G. R. French. The institution has grown steadily in deposits and in favor in the community since its organization. During the panic of 1893 the Bank would no doubt have been compelled to suspend business during that year, but for the fact that Mr. H. Walters, of the Atlantic Coast Line, guaranteed all depositors against any loss and provided funds in Baltimore to pay all depositors in full. Since that time the growth of the Bank in deposits and prosperity has been much more rapid than at any previous time in its history. The deposits now exceed $200,000, the surplus account $5,000, and the stock sells readily at 20 per cent. premium. The policy of the Directors of this Company is to strengthen the Bank financially in every conceivable way. J. W. Norwood is President, H. Walters Vice-President and George Sloan Cashier.

CAPE FEAR LUMBER CO.

One of the largest manufacturers of kiln-dried North Carolina pine lumber in the rough is the Cape Fear Lumber Company. Having a double band mill, about twenty million feet of lumber can be made each year. Recently the Company was re-organized by electing E. C. Gates President, and Bradley L. Eaton Secretary and Treasurer, both residing in New York; and John A. Arringdale, Vice-Pesident and General Manager, who resides here. The entire product of these mills is handled in New York City and Eastern markets, and is shipped mostly by water.

ELEVATOR AND FERTILIZING WAREHOUSES.

The Wilmington Compress and Warehouse Company own the Elevator and Storage Warehouses, which are separated from their cotton warehouses by the saw mills of J. H. Chadbourn & Co. Here guano, kainit, salt and other products in bulk are received from vessels and stored in bulk. This plant is fitted with Hunt's patent elevator and engine, the most rapid method known for discharging cargo in bulk, vessels frequently discharging two hundred and fifty tons in ten hours, the material being dumped in a hopper, thence loaded in cars and dropped from elevated railroad into the bins below.

S. H. FISHBLATE.

The attractive clothing and furnishing store of S. H. Fishblate may be mentioned as one of the largest and most complete emporiums of its kind in the State. The proprietor came to this city in 1869 and began business on Market street. In 1879 he moved to his present quarters, Nos. 22 & 24 North Front street, where he carries the largest stock in his line in the State. He is sole agent for Dunlap's celebrated hat, pearl shirts and

Strouse & Bros'., "high art" clothing. Mr. Fishblate is public-spirited and progressive, and has been prominent in municipal affairs for many years, serving on the Board of Aldermen for six terms and Mayor for four terms. He recently resigned this high office, and now devotes his entire time to his business, which he intends shall make his name even more widely known than through the channels of political ambition.

HALL & PEARSALL.

Some of our best citizens have been given to us by the old county of Duplin, which was also the home of both members of the above firm— Messrs. B. F. Hall and Oscar Pearsall. The senior member is one of the many Duplin county veterans of four year's service in the Confederate Army, for which the junior member was ineligible on account of his youth. But now, thirty years after the war, they are both veterans among the mercantile firms of this city.

The business was established at No. 3 South Water street in the year 1869 by J. J. Edwards and B. F. Hall. Increasing trade called for larger room, and about the year 1873 they bought and occupied the large brick building on the same street, in which they did a prosperous business till the death of Mr. Edwards in the year 1876. On his death the firm name was changed to Hall & Pearsall, Mr. Pearsall having been admitted a partner the year previous.

Under the favorable conditions then existing the new firm continued to do a prosperous and increasing business in the old stand until the year 1892, when they moved into the store and offices (which they still occupy) in the large new building on the corner of Nutt and Mulberry streets. And in order to utilize the large property owned by them on the river-front between the depots of the A. C. Line and the Seaboard Air Line, a large wharf was extended to deep water, with a commodious dock on each side, and on the property two large warehouses were built and connected by private lines with the different railroad depots of the city.

In this shipping depot, called "Waterland," they carry a large stock of heavy goods, such as salt, meats, flour, molasses, fish, bagging, ties, nails, iron, etc., which they are able to ship either by water or rail at the least expense of handling. In their store and offices on Front street they exhibit samples of their heavy stock, together with a full line of light goods, selected chiefly with reference to the requirements of the country trade.

The firm owns a large storage depot on Point Peter, at the junction of the Cape Fear and North East rivers, where their receipts of naval stores and produce of that class are handled by competent men employed for the purpose.

WILMINGTON REFRIGERATOR AND ICE WORKS

W. E. Worth & Co., proprietors of the Wilmington Refrigerator and Ice Works, have the most extensive and complete plant of the kind in the State. At their large Ice Factory, with a capacity of forty tons per day, they manufacture hygeinic ice, as near absolutely pure as can be made artificially. They give special attention to orders for one hundred and two hundred pounds. And ice by the car-load is loaded direct from the Ice House to the cars without being exposed to either the sun or air, thus avoiding loss in leakage thereby. Undoubtedly their facilities for doing a general ice business, in all its details, are unsurpassed, and the quality of the ice is the very best. They solicit orders. The managing partner, Mr. William E. Worth, one of the most honored names in the State, has long experience in this business. He is, perhaps, without any exception, "the greatest hustler in Wilmington," and it is said one must be an early riser to get ahead of him. Besides his management here, he is interested in the same line of business at Goldsboro, Rocky Mount and Greensboro, and is Director in several companies organized for the material development of the State.

ARMOUR PACKING COMPANY.

This is a branch of Armour Packing Company, of Kansas City, the largest Packing House in the world. All kinds of fresh and cured meats, in refrigerator cars, owned and operated by the company, are received almost daily. A large cold storage room, for the purpose of keeping beef, pork, mutton and sausage fresh and sweet, is kept at a temperature of 35° all the year round.

A large stock of all kinds of dry, salt and smoked meats constantly on hand. Hams and breakfast bacon, including the famous "Gold Band" brand, "White Label," and "Helmet" pure leaf lard, and Helmet brand canned meats. Ships, railroads and commissaries supplied with barrel beef, and pork, oils and tallow. All orders filled promptly from this branch. Pure animal fertilizers sold in any quantity. Correspondence solicited.

L. P. MacKenzie is Manager of the branch at Wilmington, N. C.

WILMINGTON IRON WORKS.

This corporation has been identified with Wilmington industries for more than half a century. The firm was originally Polley & Hart, then Hart & Bailey, then Burr & Bailey, from which it was changed a few years ago to the Wilmington Iron Works. Mr. H. A. Burr and Mr. E. P. Bailey, the proprietors, need no introduction, being well-known as technical and practical engineers, honored citizens and energetic thrifty business men. They describe their works as architectural and general foundry, machine shops, wood work, sash, doors, &c. Copper stills, machinery supplies. Agency of leading houses in belting, Engines, Gins, &c., located at Nos. 19 and 21 South Front Street.

XLVI

POWELL & CO.

Powell & Co., Purveyors, have their Parlor Market at the City market. Everybody knows Sam Powell, and Sam knows everybody's appetite, and just how to meet it more than half way with a delicious, juicy steak, an artistic bundle of lamb chops, a roast that brings the smile of satisfaction to the most chronic dyspeptic and—well, just ask Sam what you want, and if he don't produce it instantly, you may as well wait, as you will not find it elsewhere. Special attention given to ship supplies. Powell & Co. get their supplies direct from the great stock centre of America, and if there is anything good to be had Sam is not the man to be without it.

CAPE FEAR & YADKIN VALLEY RAILWAY.

Fifty years ago Fayetteville controlled nearly all the inland trade of North Carolina, with a large part of portions of Tennessee and Virginia. The merchants of Wilmington were accumulating fortunes in plying a vast and lucrative business with the West Indies; and the Cape Fear River transportation of molasses, sugar, salt, iron, coffee and the goods of the Northern markets to Fayetteville, the head of navigation, was immense. Canvas-topped wagons, drawn by two, four and six horses, with jingling bells traversing hundreds of miles from across the Blue Ridge, winding over the red hills of the rugged country about the Pilot and the Sauratown Mountains creaked slowly and heavily on, to the shout of driver and the crack of whip, towards Fayetteville, the Mecca of trade, the El Dorado of marvelous riches in merchandise. These wagons, all laden, were driven into town in long lines, grouping themselves about the different places of trade. Thence came the hum of traffic all day and often far into the night. But the "iron horse" was more powerful than the road-wagon, and for this cause Fayetteville lost most of her back country trade.

In 1852 a charter was granted for the Western (Coal Fields) Railroad, extending from Fayetteville West, through the counties of Cumberland,

XLVII

Moore, Harnett and Chatham, which, with the large amount of stock taken therein by the State, and by the aid of liberal subscriptions from the county of Cumberland, the town of Fayetteville and individual stockholders, was built to Egypt, progressing no farther than that point when the outbreak of the war suspended all further operations. Imperfectly worked as they were, the coal mines of Egypt and the Western Railroad, with its facilities for transportation, proved of incalculable service to the Confederate Government in the struggle of four years which ensued.

As far back as 1815 the immense advantages of opening to the markets of the world the rich territory of the Upper Yadkin Valley by connection with Fayetteville as the head of navigation on the Cape Fear River had attracted the attention of leading men in the Legislature, and such connection by canal was favorably reported and even undertaken, but the obstacles opposing themselves proved insurmountable to the crude progress of that day, and the work was abandoned.

Later, in the late 40's and early 50's, Edward Lee Winslow, George McNeill, H. L. Myrover, T. S. Lutterloh, A. A. McKethan, D. A. Ray, Jonathan Worth, G. Deming, John H. Hall, Duncan G. McRae, Alexander Murchison, Daniel McDiarmid and others, under charter, built the Fayetteville & Western Plank Road in order to reach the rich and productive sections of Western Carolina. These public-spirited men went to work to tear away the veil which had so long covered their eyes and blinded them to their interests, and relieve from the bondage in which the people of the productive region of Western Carolina had been kept by bad roads. This means of transportation was some relief, giving a quicker and more healthful circulation through the arteries of trade. But these roads were not adapted to the wants and conditions of the people, and the attention of all was directed to the feasibility of building the Western Railroad.

Whilst all who based their conclusions upon a knowledge of the country to be penetrated by the Western Railroad rested in a full conviction of its vast importance and of its ultimate final triumph, yet there was a number whose minds were closed against such conviction, and who, with triumphant air, proclaimed its uselessness and prophesied its failure. These

XLVIII

evil declarations and ill-timed prophecies were not the fault of the country which was to be reached, or for any want of great and mighty resources within it, but only the misfortune of ignorance on the part of the prophets and their own utter want, in this behalf, of any resources whatever. That any one born in North Carolina could have permitted himself to doubt or declare disbelief in the importance and success of a railway communication through the great Yadkin Valley, furnishes only melancholy evidence of the inexplicable conclusions to which human judgment will arrive. That this Valley should have been so long neglected was a riddle and a wonder. That it should now, in the meridian of this enlightened century and the noon-tide of human enterprise and progress, find resistance, or indifference, or aught else than active, restless and united zeal for its development, baffles all human reason.

By the public spirit and energy of Messrs. John D. Williams, E. J. Lilly and John M. Rose and others of Fayetteville, the mists of prejudice and ignorance had to yield to the sunlight of truth.

For fourteen years the Western Railroad, although first in importance to the agricultural and commercial interests of the State had been neglected, and, indeed, lost sight of. It presented only an isolated line, without any outlet, either North or South, East or West.

But in 1879 this great proposed system of State internal improvement and material development demanded recognition and received it at the hands of the General Assembly, which, by an Act ratified February 25th, 1879, authorized the consolidation of the Western Railroad with the Mount Airy Railroad, and changed the name of the Corporation to that of Cape Fear & Yadkin Valley Railway Company.

In 1883, at the next General Assembly the State surrendered her interest in the Road, with some needed concessions, to a Company of private citizens, who went to work building wisely and vigorously.

Immediately after the new management of the Railroad, this Company entered into a contract with the Directory of the Fayetteville & Florence Railroad for the extension over its graded road-bed of the Cape Fear & Yadkin Valley to Maxton and continuing on to the State line. Simultaneously the work of construction was pushed Westward, and in 1884 trains were running into Greensboro and the Southern extension was completed to Maxton.

In 1883, a contract was made with the Directors of the Southern Pacific Railway for grading, track-laying and equipping that Road from the State line to Bennettsville, South Carolina, which work was completed in December, 1884. There was little pause in the work of extension, and in 1888 the Road was completed to Mount Airy—"the beautiful village lying under the shadow of the towering chain of the Blue Ridge." In the meantime branch roads were completed to Millboro' and Madison.

In 1890, the line was extended from Fayetteville to Wilmington, the eastern terminus. The Company immediately made their terminal facilities at Point Peter first-class, with ample accommodations for the handling of freight and passengers to the city wharves of the Company.

The work of construction was formed by the North State Improvement Company, incorporated in 1883, of which the late Mr. John D. Williams was President, and all cheerfully bear witness to the fidelity with which the work was done.

The Cape Fear & Yadkin Valley Railway crosses the chief water-ways of the State and forms a direct line through some of the finest regions of the three geological divisions of North Carolina—bisects it from northwest to southeast, aiming to make final connection by the shortest route with the great railway highway at Cincinnati and combining finally that most admirable feature of railroading which reaches out and penetrates the undeveloped back country, with its own seaport for an outlet, with all its advantages to hundreds of miles of interior of its shipping, diversified manufactures and commerce.

It will be noted that the Cape Fear & Yadkin Valley Railway system—conceived in the days of the wealth and prosperity of the tide-water and Upper Cape Fear section—lays the steel rail upon the disused old rut of this remunerative traffic, and its long trains bound with the swift life of steam power over the route of the slow-toiling wagon caravan; from the

L

seacoast to the mountains, through some of the best settlements and most fertile counties of the State, it will move still onward, signalizing the wisdom which had seized upon what nature had blazed out for a great highway of commerce.

This railway is an enduring monument of the enterprise of John D. Williams and E. J. Lilly, of Fayetteville; George W. Williams, of Wilmington; K. M. Murchison, of New York; John M. Worth, of Ashboro; W. A. Lash, of Walnut Cove; Charles P. Stokes, of Richmond, Virginia; W. A. Moore, of Mount Airy; J. Turner Morehead, of Leaksville; Robert T. Gray, of Raleigh; D. W. C. Benbow and Julius A. Gray, of Greensboro; and richly deserved all the benefits and prosperity which it should have conferred on them.

Unfortunately, the Cape Fear & Yadkin Valley Railway became embarrassed on account of its original debt of construction, bondholders became exacting for their annual interest; and, although the management avoided making any outlays of money, not absolutely necessary to be made, and the operating expenses were conducted with prudence and strict economy, the Company was forced into the hands of a receiver. General John Gill was appointed, and is at present serving in this position.

The truth is emphatic that whether in war or in peace—in the rapid transmission of troops and munitions of war to the protection of the largest seaport in the State, and therefore the most likely to be assailed, or in the commercial interchange of the products of the West for those of foreign countries, the Cape Fear & Yadkin Valley Railway is of vital importance to our State, and as such the bondholders must conclude, governed by an enlightened policy, and disregarding the sectional prejudices attempted to be excited, that it is unwise to entertain terms looking to the disposal of its divisions and thus dismembering the main line.

Upon a review of the increasing popularity of the Road, with its present connections and its increased revenue, the people of the Cape Fear section indulged the confident belief that it is destined to succeed and prosper in despite of the obstacles and difficulties it has encountered.

The energy and zeal with which Captain W. E. Kyle, General Freight and Passenger Agent, has labored for the success of the Cape Fear & Yadkin Valley Railway amid many difficulties, the fidelity he has evinced in his sphere, and his warm co-operation in all efforts to promote the progress of his Road, entitles him to the highest commendation.

Captain T. C. James, the Agent of the Cape Fear & Yadkin Valley Railway, at Wilmington, by his steadiness and attention to business, his courtesy to the patrons of his line, his zeal in the discharge of his duty, his uprightness of purpose and integrity of character, has gained him the confidence of our citizens.

HOLMES & WATTERS.

This well-known enterprising firm of young men, "native and to the manner born," needs no introduction on the Cape Fear, for their fathers and grandfathers and great-grandfathers were eminent men in its history, and the race is not dying out. The partners, Gabriel Holmes and Joseph H. Watters, served their time as grocers clerks in the fine store which they have occupied for years as principals, and they are familiar with all the details of a business which now commands, perhaps, the most extensive retail trade in Wilmington, and a large share of the wholesale business in their line. The firm stands high financially and socially, and they attend strictly to their business.

SNEED & CO.

Invite an inspection of their stock of furniture, carpets and matting, house-furnishings and window-shades. They are also large mattress manufacturers, and claim to be the cheapest furniture house in North Carolina. Their place of business is Nos. 114 and 116 Market street.

J. W. MURCHISON,

One of the most prominent hardware dealers in the State, carries a large stock of general supplies in his line, which he offers at close prices. He has the benefit of ample means and long experience in the trade, having been engaged in the business for many years, and he is generally recognized as one of the most industrious and deserving merchants in Wilmington. Call on him for agricultural implements, builders' hardware, turpentine distillers' supplies, fishing tackle, sporting goods, pistols, guns, ammunition, table and personal cutlery, and all the domestic et ceteras usually found in a first-class hardware store.

Mr Murchison and his efficient staff are the embodiment of politeness and attention. His establishment is in the heart of the city, next to the Orton Hotel.

THE NATIONAL BANK OF WILMINGTON.

This bank was incorporated in June, 1894, with a capital of $100,000. The building occupied by this bank is on the Northwest corner of Front and Princess streets, and was built by a former banking institution for this express purpose, is three stories with basement, imposing in architectural design, and admirably arranged for the safe and expeditious transaction of business.

The surplus and profits is $12,000. It is the State and County depository, and transacts a general banking business. Solicits accounts of out-of-town customers and offers every facility of first-class banking.

Mr John S Armstrong, the President, is a financier of ability, and to him is due much of the credit of establishing this bank.

Messrs. Jas. H. Chadbourn, Jr., and William Calder, the Vice-Presidents, are ever alive to the best interests of the bank, to which much of their attention is given which has resulted in making many friends and considerable business.

Mr. F. R. Hawes, the Acting Cashier, is a young man of recognized ability, thoroughly understands the business and is generally liked by the commercial people.

The directors of the bank are John S. Armstrong, Jas. H. Chadbourn, Jr., William Calder, William Gilchrist, Gabriel Holmes, C. W. Yates, George R. French, Hugh MacRae, J. G. L. Geischen, Chas. E. Borden.

KIDDER'S SAW MILL.

This establishment is the oldest, and perhaps the most extensive of its kind in Wilmington. It was owned first about the year 1834 by Captain Gilbert Potter, who operated it successfully under his own name, and who subsequently took in partnership his son-in-law, the late Mr. Edward Kidder.

The firm of Potter & Kidder was succeeded by Kidder & Martin, and after many years the name was changed to that of Edward Kidder & Sons. For more than half a century it was guided and controlled by the late Mr. Edward Kidder, honored and respected as one of Wilmington's foremost public-spirited citizens, the father of the present proprietor, Mr. George Wilson Kidder.

The present firm, Edward Kidder's Son, sustains the high reputation of its past history and controls a large trade with the West Indies.

WILMINGTON STEAM LAUNDRY.

Is owned and operated by Harper & Pennington, fully equipped with all modern appliances for cleansing wearing apparel, and other cotton, silk or woollen fabrics in the most approved manner at moderate charges. This establishment illustrates the Darwinian theory "the survival of the fittest" inasmuch as it outlived all competitors and secured the confidence of the public. A glance at their methods and neatly attired employees gives assurance of accuracy, carefulness, neatness and despatch.

S. & W. H. NORTHROP.

The business of this firm was established many years ago by Isaac Northrop, now deceased, father of the present proprietors. These gentlemen, who were brought up in the lumber business, have a large experience in this trade and have successfully conducted it for a period of many years.

Their mill, drying kilns and yards are conveniently situated on the river in the Southern part of the city, and everything connected with their plant is thoroughly equipped with the latest improved methods, to save expense and expedite business.

They are large exporters of all kinds of lumber.

Both members of this firm take an active part in everything that pertains to the lumber interest of Wilmington and the material development of the city.

CAROLINA COOPERAGE AND VENEER CO.

This Company was organized June 1, 1894, for the purpose of manufacturing oil, spirits of turpentine and syrup barrels, also crates, baskets and all the various packages for truckers. All these goods are manufactured from North Carolina timber and are superior in make and finish to any imported stock. In the manufacture of barrels they have patented machinery of a capacity of a barrel per minute. Their extensive plant, which occupies a whole block, located between the Atlantic Coast Line and the Seaboard Air Line depots, is complete in all its details. R. M. Nimocks, of Fayetteville, is President, and E. M. Wells is Manager.

W. F. KETCHUM,

Manufacturer and dealer in buggies, wagons, carts, drays, etc., at corner Second and Princess streets, solicits orders, guaranteeing excellent work and satisfactory prices.

CALIFORNIA FRUIT TRANSPORTATION CO.

Some ten years ago the California Fruit Transportation Company began its career with fifty-five of their celebrated cars, carrying fruit and vegetables from Mississippi, Tennessee and Southern Illinois to Chicago for F. A. Thomas & Son, and were operated by Messrs. Thomas & Son.

The usefulness and great success of these cars made it apparent that the new field just then opening in California demanded such facilities, and to market its fruits successfully in Eastern markets, 200 cars were built and put into the service. From that time the demand has so increased that the Company has now 1,000 cars in service, transporting fruits from and to all sections of the United States.

In 1892 there was a demand for California fruits across the water, and the Company, ever alive to the fruit industries, made arrangements to carry California fruits to Liverpool, England, using and fitting up the White Star Line steamers Majestic and Teutonic. Liverpool, however, not proving a desirable market, the Company turned its attention to London, and arranged to put California fruits into that city in fourteen days. By the use of special export trains across the Continent, transferring at New York into the magnificent steamers, of the American Line, Paris, New York, St. Louis and St. Paul, carrying the fruit in cold storage and delivering into the London market in perfect condition, the fruit has always sold for good prices.

In this section of North Carolina the California Fruit Transportation Company is building up an industry which is assuming immense proportions. During the year 1892 this Company moved from Wilmington and intermediate stations to Goldsboro, on the line of the Wilmington and Weldon Railroad, to Northern and Eastern markets, 43 cars with 7,465 crates, of 32 quarts each, or 238,880 quarts of strawberries. This year (1896) they have moved 290 cars from this section with 81,000 crates, or 2,602,000 quarts, of berries and 1,300 packages of vegetables.

The vegetable and strawberry business is on the increase, not only in this section, but in all parts of the Southern States, and it is through the energy of A. S. Maynard, Southern Agent, and his able assistant, C. W. Woodward, backed by their Company through its General Manager, H. A. Thomas, that, with a good refrigerator service, this Line has been able to accomplish these good results and give such general satisfaction to the growers.

The officers of the California Fruit Transportation Company are: F. A. Thomas, President; E. R. Hutchins, Vice-President; H. A. Thomas, General Manager, and W. H. Hubbard, Secretary and Treasurer. The general offices are located at No. 904, "The Rookery Building, Chicago, Illinois.

Mr. H. A. Thomas, the General Manager, is a gentleman of pronounced ability, who has successfully operated this Line from the beginning and established a business of so large proportions. He is always actively engaged in working for the material advancement of shippers of fruits and vegetables.

Mr. A. S. Maynard, the Southern Agent, is a leading spirit in Transportation circles, ever on the alert, polite and considerate to all, and ever alive to the development of his Company and the progress of its patrons.

Mr. Charles Worth Woodward, Assistant Southern Agent, has all his life been engaged in the ice business, and having had the experience so necessary to a full realization of the importance of proper refrigeration, is an acquisition to the corps of able officials. He is becoming one of the prime factors in the growth and prosperity of the California Fruit Transportation Company.

S. L. ALDERMAN,

The photographer, has his gallery at No. 119½ Market Street. His work is executed in the best style, and he carries in stock, for sale, views of Wilmington and vicinity. He invites all lovers of art and those desiring photographs to call at his gallery.

J. H. BOATWRIGHT & SON,

Insurance Agents, represent fire, life, boiler, accident, bond and liability insurance. Their office is at No. 124 North Water Street. Telephone No. 73.

R. F HAMME,

More familarly known as "Hamme the Hatter," can be found at his old stand, No. 26 North Front Street. For seasonable and fashionable hats he excels.

GEORGE DARDEN,

Watchmaker and Jeweler, Front Street, deals in watches, clocks and jewelry. He makes a specialty of repairing fine complicated watches, clocks and jewelry, and re-setting precious stones, and gold and silver-hand soldering. Mr. Darden is chief inspector of watches for the Wilmington, Newbern & Norfolk Railway, and division inspector for the Seaboard Air Line.

SOUTHERLAND & COWAN,

Proprietors of the large livery and sales stables, located at 108 and 110 North Second Street, between Princess and Chestnut, are prepared to give prompt attention to all calls day or night. They have first-class equipages and polite drivers. Special attention given to boarding horses—box stalls, and careful grooming for trotting horses. Hacks and baggage line to all trains going and coming. These gentlemen have on hand everything in the harness and horse-dressing line. Their telephone is No. 15.

H. C. PREMPERT'S SONS.

Messrs. Arthur and Al. G. Prempert comprising the firm, are practical barbers and hair-cutters. Their work is done in the latest and most approved styles. They can be found at No. 11 South Front Street.

SOL. BEAR,
(Established 1853.)

Long and favorably known to the trade, has his extensive establishment on Market, between Front and Water Streets. He offers at wholesale dry goods. Retail, carpets, oil cloth, mattings, house-furnishing goods, etc.

D. McEACHERN.

Mr. Duncan McEachern has a good name to start with; he comes of that sturdy race of Scotch ancestors who settled on the Upper Cape Fear, and who brought with them strong arms, honest hearts and the principles of an abiding faith in God, which govern these faithful people. Mr. McEachern has an extensive up country business, originally built up by Woody & Currie, whom he succeeded. He is a factor and general commission merchant, attentive to his business, and thoroughly reliable in every respect.

P. HEINSBERGER, Jr.,

Book-seller and Stationer, also dealer in fine pictures, fancy goods, wedding presents, dolls, toys. All kinds of musical instruments, base-ball goods and hammocks, and agent for Williams' Typewriter. He can be found at 107 Market Street.

H. E. BONITZ,

Architect and Superintendent, has his office at 129 Market Street. He has displayed untiring energy and superior talent, and is gaining quite a reputation for artistic work and faithful execution of work entrusted to him.

DIVINE & CHADBOURN.

These progressive young merchants occupy the store formerly "Daggett's Old Stand," No. 23 Market street. They carry a full line of paints, oils, glass, sash, doors and blinds. Machinery and burning oils, copper paints and paints for exposure to salt atmosphere a specialty. They deal in the best and are fast gaining a large local business, as well as an extensive out-of-town trade.

JAMES D. DRY,

Proprietor of the Steam Cleaning and Dyeing Establishment, No. 16 North Second street. He is prepared to do a superior quality of dyeing on ladies' dresses and gentlemen's suits, Surah silks and kid gloves. Dry cleaning and fine dyeing given prompt and careful attention

RICHARDS & KING,

Photo-Engravers and Designers, are ready to execute promptly and reasonably all commissions in their line of work. The illustrations and designs of this book have been prepared by them and testify to their capabilities.

Both of the partners are alert, industrious, thrifty and courteous, and business entrusted to them will always receive prompt and careful attention

H. A. TUCKER & BRO.

Owners of Granite and Marble Works, at 310 North Front Street, are prepared to furnish designs on application and promptly execute, in the best workmanship, all orders entrusted to them.

M. P. TAYLOR, Jr., & CO.,

Proprietors of the Bicycle Parlors, corner Second and Market streets, keep on hand the following Wheels: The Solid Sterling—built like a watch; Tribune—a gentleman's mount; Monarch—king of bicycles; Dayton—a wheel of beauty; Eclipse—the strong wheel; Marvel, Defiance, Apollo, at prices ranging from $35 to $100. All kinds of repairing, enameling and vulcanizing. New wheels to rent exclusively to the white trade. They also deal in Electric Fans.

R. H. GRANT,

Plumber and Gas Fitter, No. 119 North Front street. Sanitary plumbing a specialty. Full stock of plumbing and gas fitting on hand. Bath-tubs, ranges, globes, hose, slate mantels, grates and stoves. Hot water, steam-heating and tin-roofing.

A. D. BROWN,

Successor to Brown & Roddick, has been established in business in this city for over a quarter of a century. He is located in a well-arranged building (No. 29 North Front street), adapted to the requirements of his trade, which is known as the Dry Goods and Carpet House of Wilmington.

J. HICKS BUNTING,

The Druggist, can be found in the Young Men's Christian Association Building, o: North Front, between Grace and Walnut streets. He carries a full line of drugs, etc., and gives prompt and careful attention to filling prescriptions.

THE REAL ESTATE INVESTMENT COMPANY OF WILMINGTON, NORTH CAROLINA,

Has a paid-up capital of $75,000. It owns and has fully paid for 80,000 acres of land in Hyde and Tyrrell counties, including the celebrated tract known as

Hyde Park,

which Prof. Holmes, the State Geologist, who personally surveyed it, says is "very valuable for agricultural purposes, unequaled as a cattle range, unexcelled as a game preserve, as many as 26 deer having been started in a single day. The standing and buried timber is also of great value."

The Company also hold options on all State lands and invites correspondence of persons seeking investments. Thomas W. Strange President. William H. Sprunt Secretary and Treasurer.

W. N. CRONLY,
Notary Public, Wilmington, N. C., by Appointment of His Excellency Governor Carr.

May be seen in all business hours at the Office of Alexander Sprunt and Son, prepared to attest contracts or any other legal writings within the purview of his commission.

STEAM TUG MARION.

THE DIAMOND STEAMBOAT AND WRECKING COMPANY.

The Diamond Steamboat and Wrecking Company was incorporated several years ago, supplying a want the requirement of which had been very seriously felt by the commercial interests of the port of Wilmington. This Company own the splendid tug "Marion," two powerful hoisters, pile-drivers, diving apparatus and all the appliances necessary for towing, loading and unloading vessels, building wharves, executing operations under the surface of the water, and, in fact, are thoroughly equipped to do all kinds of work that the name of the Company indicates. Captain Edgar D. Williams is Manager.

JAS. H. CHADBOURN & CO.

The oldest firm without change in Wilmington, if not in the State, and one of the most prominent and successful.

Their saw mill is fully equipped with the best methods and processes of manufacturing lumber known to modern science, and the best of experienced skill is brought to bear in every department. Their lumber yard commands a large general trade and their special orders attest the high standing of their carefully selected material.

The original members of the firm James H. Chadbourn and George Chadbourn, came here in early life, and by strict economy, attention to business, sobriety and industry, made a reputation for business integrity and Christian benevolence. Mr. George Chadbourn died in 1891. His munificent gifts for church and other purposes were evidences of his true merit.

Although the firm is still continued under the name of James H. Chadbourn & Co., the milling lumber and shingle business is conducted under the corporate name of the Chadbourn Lumber Company, the officers being James H. Chadbourn, President; J. H. Chadbourn, Jr., Secretary and Treasurer, and W. H. Chadbourn, Manager.

PRESS NOTICES

* * * There is in addition to the traditional features much historical information in these papers here presented in attractive form. The book is clearly printed illustrated, handsomely bound and will make an valuable addition to the library.—Morning Star (Wilmington).

Mr. Sprunt has related the incidents of early Colonial history and the later events of the Civil War in his usual graphic manner, and the book will prove interesting reading to all who take pride in our history, and will be a valuable reference book to the student.—Southport Leader.

Our thanks are due to the author, Mr. James Sprunt, of Wilmington, N. C., for a copy of a really charming little puplication entitled "Tales and Traditions of the Lower Cape Fear," giving the past, present and possible future of that section. The name and reputation of the author afford the best evidence of the attractiveness and real value of the work.—The Robesonian (Lumberton).

LXIV

James Sprunt, Esq., of Wilmington, has put forth an exceedingly attractive little paper back book—not such a very little one, either, for it is of about 300 pages—entitled "Tales and Traditions of the Lower Cape Fear, 1661-1896." Its style is delightfully fresh and chatty, and a glance shows that the volume is not confined to the telling of tales, but is in a sense a history of the historically interesting lower Cape Fear section.- Charlotte Observer.

* * * * * * * Captain J. W. Harper's picture, and that of his fine steamer, very appropriately are in the first place of the book, and to-day no pleasanter trip can be made than on this steamer, which is commanded by the universally popular Captain John W Harper.—Newbern Journal.

"Tales and Traditions of Lower Cape Fear is a very charming book. The writer of this note has a special fondness for persons and things of the olden time, and more and more as the years go by that are fast numbering him among them. This book then that brings to him most vividly the things that he has seen, the persons he has known, the very many things of which he has heard and not a few of which he has never conceived all true, all interesting, all valuable, as history rescued from the oblivion into which it has almost disappeared is most highly prized It is not a book to devour, but a book to luxuriate upon at leisure. How delightful on the broad piazza of a summer home, the broad ocean stretching out before one, while the cooling breeze refreshes the fevered brow, and the low murmur of the waves as they lash the shore soothes and calm the care worn spirit, to read of the scenes which were almost in full view of the spot where one is sitting. In view, indeed, of the very spot where lay the Federal fleet when Fort Fisher fell, and full in sight of the course over which the fleet blockade-runners spe d when pursued by their foes

A charming book it is. The author has spared no pains to obtain the facts, and in this and in presentatoin of them he gives full credit to those who have imparted them. In general the style, as is appropriate, is simple without the least attempt at ornament, but again. as occasion requires, there are passages of elevated thought and rhythmic expression that add zest to the feast of which the reader is partaking. The book is well printed by Messrs. LeGwin Bros.—North Carolina Presbyterian

"Tales and Traditions of the Lower Cape Fear, 1661-1896," by Mr. James Sprunt, of this city, is a really interesting, instructive and valuable contribution not only to the history and romantic incidents of this section but to North Carolina history. It contains much to entertain, and shows how a diligent explorer and a competent writer can gather forgotten and practically lost material, and so utilize it as to make it a positive source of pleasure and profit. The little volume contains over 2 0 pages, and is dedicated to the memory of the late Hon. George Davis in apt, felicitous phrasing that says not a word too much. The "little guide book" was prepared in six weeks, but it is well done and deserves many readers. Such a book has been long needed, and we are glad that Mr. Sprunt has taken the time to prepare it and so well Dr. Kingsbury in Wilmington Messenger.

www.ingramcontent.com/pod-product-compliance
Lightning Source LLC
Chambersburg PA
CBHW031934230426
43672CB00010B/1924